For The Jons, Steaders, Matty Mat Mat, the Higgs, Graham, Pete, Hebe, my parents and Lucy. Beautiful reasons to swim harder than I've swam before.

It's weird. When I got hit by a car when I was nineteen the impact threw me in the air and I vividly remember thinking: "So that's what it's like to be hit by a car." As if I'd always imagined what it'd be like and now I had confirmation.

Anyway, right now I'm definitely drowning, and it is nothing like I expected.

STARING DEATH IN THE FACE

Searching For The Reaper Across Mexico

Danny Smith

1. Catch your Death

Heathrow is a hinterland, a space between spaces with gates and paths and roads and entrances and exits that open and close seemingly on the whim of a capricious god

"Where are you going?" The liftshare driver has a strong accent but is enunciating his way through it deliberately.

"Errm Terminal 4. I thought the app thing told you?" I'm flummoxed after being dropped off at the wrong terminal, and spending the next 45 minutes panicking, all the while carrying a bag approximately the size of a small mom.

"No man, where are you flying to?"

"Oh sorry, I'm going to Mexico."

"Nice. Holiday?" He seems determined to earn his five stars, or just likes talking to people.

"Not really. Off to find Death," I say. There is a pause.

"Death?"

"Yeah," I say, "I want to have a word."

****

My room is stuffed with what's left of everything I own, recklessly culled to fit into my dad's car before he drove us five hours back. Forty years on this planet with only a box of books and a few black bin liners of clothes. I don't have it in me to unpack. And I

couldn't stay in the room. So I've crawled out onto the roof with some beer and Señor Carpenter.

Picking up my stuff very much felt like the full stop to the last eight years. But I'm nowhere near the capital letter of a new sentence. The love I felt turned to cotton wool in my head, full, numb. That's why I've come out to my roof - the room, and my head, are too full.

The beer isn't cold but my fingers are. The roof is in shadow. I can see the sun creep across the gardens of my parents' neighbours as it starts to set on one of these bright but biting early autumn evenings. It's becoming increasingly difficult to pull the knots out of Señor Carpenter's strings. No matter how careful I am, they always get tangled during any move. Maybe it's the stress.

I don't know when I got Señor Carpenter. He's certainly from before I met Her and, although tangled and dirty, he's still here. Señor Carpenter is a marionette puppet of a skeleton. I've always called him that because he looks a little bit Mexican and a little bit like Karen Carpenter. A marionette puppet lasted longer than the love of my life.

I'm trying not to think about starting again, or anything really - thinking and feeling hurt. I'm focusing on his skeleton head. I know this string is normally loose. When you pull it the head rises up on the other string. But every twist I untwist and line I unknot makes it seem further broken. Like quicksand, the more I struggle the deeper I sink.

I've thrown him out of my reach by the edge of the roof. Why bother? He'll just get twisted again. Everything ends. Why start if you're going to have to stop? I've accidentally drunk all my lager and it's getting colder. But if I go inside there are the failure bags and the memories that cling to them like cobwebs. I look over at Señor Carpenter, a broken twisted thing.

I want to fix him. I could fix him. It'd take me completely disman-tling him and possibly restringing him. I've done it before but I don't see the point now. Maybe he should just do everyone a favour and fall off the roof?

Everything ends. Death's grinning head has a permanent smile, fixed and mocking. What would he say? Not Señor Carpenter, but his twin, Mr Death. What would I say if I met him? When I meet him? Fuck him. Somebody should do something, say something. It's not fair. Working so hard and everything just ending. He needs to be told. I wiggle over to my puppet, the tiles move and crack as they take my weight.

I can't fix him, not yet. Not until I know. Not until I've had a word. I'm going to find Mr Death and I'm going to get answers. Where? I squint at Señor Carpenter. Mexico? Mexico. Where they understand Death. A whole festival dedicated to him. Día de los Muertos, Day of the Dead.

The tiles crack just that bit more. How did I get so close to the edge? Is it windy? I'm swaying. I'm going to get answers.

If I get off this roof.

****

Check-in. The pub near my gate is still waking up even though I'm far from the first person here. Someone is flitting around setting up the menus and I can see some staff wrapping cutlery out the back. I approach the only person serving, she automatically sets up a coffee cup.

"Please may I have a pint of Heineken?" The lady pauses, takes the coffee cup away from the machine and looks at a pint glass as if it's her first time encountering one. I honestly don't feel like a pint at this point but it's important. The atemporal airport pint is a British working-class tradition. More than that, it's a ritual. A demarcation between 'normal' time rules and 'holiday' time. Saturnalia rules, where the natural order is reversed: morning drinking, afternoon naps, adults playing, kids at the adults table. All beginning with a symbolic first pint. Even though I don't really fancy it, the pint is cold and is shaking loose some of the latent airport stress.

The first flight is only an hour and as we break above the clouds I can't help but notice how much it looks like heaven, or at least peoples' cartoon idea of heaven.

If above the clouds is heaven, then airport lounges are as close to purgatory as is possible on Earth. In Charles De Gaulle the lounge is comfortably warm, but the air seems oppressive like one too many jumpers. The decor is what I would call 'fancy' but at this point I've been awake for twenty-four hours straight and I'm facing four more here in seats slightly less than comfortable enough to sleep in. I ask for tea and get a cup of water slightly less than hot enough to make a hot drink and a tea bag placed on a damp tray. I couple this with a pork wrap with slightly less taste needed to be described as 'nice', for which I pay only slightly less than a Citroen Hatchback.

The other passengers are draped across the furniture in various states of snoozing boredom. Everyone is quiet apart from the staff of the cafe who are talking in loud rough French and neither giving a monkeys if they wake anyone up or if they understand the language, judging from the odd swear word I am picking up here and there.

****

Ten hours isn't long at all. International travel is perfect for someone who's been an insomniac all their life. Not only are you immune to jet lag, well, not immune, but almost always in a state of bone tiredness and unable to sleep in rhythm with your surroundings. Also, you're able to kill long periods of time. I watch the small screen, half looking for Mr D. His bone fingers are everywhere. We seem to be insulated from all aspects of death in our real lives but our fictional worlds are rife with death. Death as motivation, death as resolution, retribution, reckoning, and even punchline.

Nearly 40 years of assimilating death in our imagination and he still has the ability to jump out from behind the door. Love is on the screen too, but disappoints. We invest so heavily in the notion, the truth and the power of love because of how it's portrayed in our stories. But love doesn't work like that. Love is sneaky. It never jumps out from behind the door. Love is there, like it has always been there when you do notice it. Dizzying and happy, like waking up and remembering you live in a theme park. I mean, really, it should be the other way round. Death is guaranteed. Love, unfortunately, isn't.

It's just getting dark by the time I've collected my bag, bought a bus ticket and left the air-conditioned airport. I have no idea if it's twilight the next day or the day before. I'm close to thirty-odd hours awake with only a couple of hours of sleep on the plane. The sky is a light blue, shading towards navy, with smears of pink and red on a few patches of cloud. There seems to be more sky here - so big it's heavy, crushing down being kept at bay by the heat and ozone in the air. What I can see of the landscape is desert scrub and the airport is modern and white.

I'm waiting for a bus in the bays outside the doors of arrivals and, naturally after what happened in India I'm nervous.

****

After 30 hours in transit from Heathrow to New Delhi via Dubai I'm spewed out into a humid dusty night with no clue how to get to my hotel. The flight landed over an hour late so it's dark and the throng of people outside the airport doors all seem completely disinterested in helping me. I head to a stand that advertises 'prepay taxis direct'. It seems legit. I might be paying a little over the odds, but I'm tired and I just changed a lot of money that's sweating in a body wallet next to my chest. I catch sight of myself in an electronic display that goes black for a second: black smudges for eyes, skin hanging off my bones and clothes that have kinda bonded to my body, gritty and folded into my skin. I'm just happy when I get a driver instead of a magic amulet smashed on my head to break the curse.

I decide I like the driver. This, of course, being after I adjust to Indian driving, which is a cross between riding the dodgems and a rollercoaster. They use the horns as communal echolocation and it seems to work. It did get a bit hairy when he stopped in the middle of a dual carriageway to close the boot that had come open after swerving sharply out of the way of another car. He asked me what job I did and I explained about the one I'd just left, to which he said "It's a good job you're fat, so kids are no problem." Not that he was particularly slim himself. He was a solidly built 'man' off the peg from the average shop. Jumper, functional jacket, that sort of thing. He got to central Delhi and drove to a dark neighbourhood, more shacks than buildings.

"I'm just going to check how to get to your hotel,' he says. "I ask these men."

"Don't you know?"

"Of course I know, but the festival I was telling you about has closed many blocks."

To be fair to him, earlier he was telling me about a festival with 'many dancing'. He goes over to talk to some men roasting rat over a fire made out of a tin can – or whatever else my white, panicky, traveller brain has pasted over the real memory. He comes back and tells me the men didn't know but he does know an 'information office' so we head there.

Inside, I meet a charming and handsome young man, tired but smiling, and wearing his uniform with the attitude of a man that finishes in an hour. We phone the hotel and the man that answers tells me they have cancelled my booking because of the festival and I will be refunded in seven days. There's nothing at the next four, then five, then six hotels. A couple of others quote figures around the equivalent of £400 for one night.

I start laughing. I honestly don't know what else to do. This confused the Tourist Information Boy into a coughing fit. He checked for any overnight trains and buses but everything has departed because it's well after 11pm at this point. Then he smiles like he's just come up with an idea. He tells me he can put me on a 'cultural exchange program' where I travel to the Himalayas for 10 days, with food, board and transfers thrown in and - the best thing is – they keep a place to put travellers up for the night before they're picked up in the morning. You stop and travel on a houseboat, and the pictures look lovely so I put it down as a possibility.

I dig around my bag for my guidebook, having run out of hotels in his. I have a quick check under 'Delhi' and the first thing I read is a warning of fake taxi drivers that take people to fake tourist information offices that try and put you on hugely inflated package tours.

It occurs to me that all the phone calls have been dialled by him and he spoke to everyone first before he passed the phone over to me. And the train timetables - I just took his word for it rather than work out what they said. This leaves me in the office of some con men in a truly foreign and frankly intimidating country, with no place to stay and outnumbered four to one, including the drunk guy in the foyer who keeps shouting "party blue" at me over the partition.

The trick, it seems, is to get out of the situation without calling them liars or being outright mugged. I tell the information guy:

"Well I'm going back to the airport, there will definitely be a hotel there." He tells me I won't be allowed back into the airport without a ticket because the police patrol the roads.

I say I don't mind, I'll just explain my situation to them and he shuts up.

****

After 20 minutes a coach pulls up and the driver gets off. Before I can work out if this is my coach or not he approaches another couple and mimes 'ticket' to them. They show a ticket and he gestures to get on with a warm flick of the head. By the time he gets to me I have my ticket ready. He tells me to get on board with that same head flick.

"Merci," I say. He pauses, the flight was Air France and I have a little French, so my brain is still there. He stops with raised eyes as if waiting for me to get it right.

"Gratzi," I say in a passable Italian accent. Shit, not that one.

"Ciao?" The driver is weirdly amused but I'm falling to pieces. Memories of a thousand resort costa del holidays I've never been on kick in.

"Gracias," I say with the thickest Birmingham accent I've ever naturally used. I look down to check if I'm wearing an obnoxious suntan and Union Jack Bermuda shorts. Thankfully, the de-evolution stopped at the accent.

"De nada," says the driver and taps my back in congratulations as I climb aboard. Entering the coach feels like setting foot on a spaceship. It's nicer than the National Express. The air conditioning welcomes me, every three or four seats a tv screen hangs from the luggage rack, and the armrests are comfortable and the right height. I don't know if the seats are allocated, so I just sit down.

A Mexican family gets on and sits opposite. One of them finds a bag. We have a conversation about whether it's my bag or not, them speaking Spanish, me not understanding and replying in English. The exchange loses nothing despite the difference. As the coach sets off the lights dim and the screens come on with a short film about how to buckle the seat belts and not smoking in the toilets. Then it starts showing Mission Impossible 3, which, although not being the most labyrinthine of plots, I find hard to follow because it's dubbed into Spanish with English subtitles (except the bits in Russian which are neither dubbed nor subtitled). To make matters worse, I lip read a hell of a lot to supplement the difficulties I have with phonics and I'm incredibly tired, which makes it look like when Tom Cruise says anything the words are floating out of his mouth and, in some weird form of synesthesia, appearing at the bottom of the screen. The drive has been mostly highway, but now we're swinging through suburbs. Every so often it's punctuated by small convenience stores, young men on the curb bathing in the only light spilling from the doors and the screens of arcade cabinets outside.

Cancún bus station. A quick peruse of the guidebook before I got off told me a fun fact: Cancún is possibly a Mayan word that translates as 'place of snakes'. Another fun fact that pops up when you Google Cancún is that its murder rate is currently three times higher than the national average. I chose Cancún to start because it's a tourist city, built for outsiders. I figured being in a part of the country designed for loud obnoxious drunk white people who speak little to no Spanish would ease the culture shock. Of course my budget didn't stretch to staying in the strip of hotels and bars surrounded by the white sands and calm waters of the Gulf of Mexico, so I'm staying in El Centro, the part of the city for the workers that provide the infrastructure for the capitalist fantasy.

The bus station at El Centro is busy tonight. In a daze I head for an exit and outside is just as busy, with street vendors selling food, cars and taxis pulling around each other in no discernible system and people wandering in between, confident of their invulnerability to cars. Before a rogue taxi driver can bamboozle me into a dodgy ride and some lightly veiled extortion, I walk away from the crowds toward the back of the bus station. Luckily, the coach station Wi-Fi works all the way up to the back wall. According to the map, the street my hostel is on is the one just to the left. It must be good luck, because it's certainly not good planning.

Checking in, I hand my passport to Julio behind the counter.

"Hey you're from Birmingham!" he says in the near perfect English that has thrown me off since I walked through the door of the hostel.

"Yes, I am. Do you know it?" I ask.

"No , not really, I know the teams, are you City or a Villa fan?" he says. Now, I stopped pretending to have an interest in football so other men felt comfortable in my presence years ago, but I like Julio, and he seems really proud of his English football knowledge.

"I come from a big family of Blues fans. They'd kill me if I didn't say Blues"

"They'd kill you?" Julio is concerned.

"No," I backtrack. "Not actually kill me. They wouldn't be happy." Julio looks a little confused. "What team do you support?" Julio lifts his work uniform shirt up to reveal a Liverpool shirt underneath and smiles.

"Reds," he says.

"I'm glad I didn't say Everton," I tell him and he smiles again. I've reached the end of my football knowledge.

"Why are you here?" asks Julio.

"Good question, I'll add it to the list."

"What?"

"Don't worry about it" I say, and quickly add "I'm here for the Día de los Muertos"

"Oh, it's not what you think" says Julio.

"What do you mean?"

"Tourists think it's a big fiesta, but it's more of a familia thing. At the hotels you can maybe wear masks to the clubs." He sees I'm disappointed. "They do fiestas in the bigger cities though, I'm pretty sure."

Luckily, he offers to give me the tour of the hostel. It's nice, or it was nice a few seasons ago, now it's a little worn around the edges. The hot tub on the roof bar is permanently broken, the murals are faded, and the floor has been mopped with bleach one too many times. But the dorm beds each have an electrical outlet and a mini fan attached to the bed frame, the lockers are massive, and the toilet has a lock on the door.

After a quick shower, I pop downstairs for the local gen on somewhere good to eat. My new friend Julio points me to the quesadilla franchise over the road. It's an open-fronted tile and concrete unit with plastic picnic furniture and an open grill. It's staffed by three ladies who laugh when I approach, but in a warm way like dinner ladies watching a dog that had wandered into the school playground. I point and mispronounce things from the menu and take a Coke from the fridge.

Sitting at the table, one of the dinner ladies comes over and asks a question about my order in Spanish I just say "si" a little too hopefully. She goes back to the others and they all laugh. I take a sip of Coke. I'm hit by a truck of sugar. Coke is different in Mexico: it tastes like maybe it's not so silly that it once contained cocaine. I'm handed my quesadillas and sit listening to sincere Mexican pop, exhaling the 5000 miles I've travelled.

Later, I'm back at the hostel at what they call the 'rooftop bar', which I suppose is accurate as far as it's on the roof and I'm drinking. It's actually the kitchen and dining area, with some communal space. I'm leaning on the wall looking at the surrounding area now it's dark. Opposite is a shoe warehouse outlet and I can see the light from two nearly identical convenience stores on opposite corners; one of them where I bought the cold Corona I'm drinking now. There are two or three sex shops I can see from here (depending on how well I'm translating the signs), a money exchange place that's still open at close to 11 at night and various abandoned shop fronts. It's a far cry from any picture that comes up when you Google 'Cancún', but the air is warm and the sky isn't 100 percent dark in the way it never is during the summer. There's no echo of the life or person I am back home, except for those in my head, and they'll be gone soon. Peace is three beers away.

I know me, I'm impulsive and easily bored; that's not to say I'm not careful though. I've discovered in any situation I've got three or four back up plans spinning themselves in the background. A luxury I wasn't aware of until now. There's a special type of panicked desperation of not having any options left. Literally nothing. Swim or die is no plan.

2. Little Black Death

Market 23 seems to be waking up as I arrive - most of the stalls seem to be selling the same sugar skull T-shirts, Cancún fridge magnets and authentic Mexican blankets. Authentic, I suspect, insofar they are actually blankets and they are being sold in Mexico. At the heart of the market is food stalls, vegetables are stacked as high as me and a butcher is busily snipping the claws off chicken feet. The smell takes me back to Birmingham's Bull Ring market and a little sprout of homesickness pushes through the heat. That smell is overpowered by the herb shop nearby - the odour of dirty liquorice and burnt vanilla. The market is empty apart from me and another white couple walking around, still a little intimidated by the area they came through to get here. They look for me and smile a smile of recognition. I obligingly give a little 'what's up' nod back.

I need a drink. My bones are aching in a definitely non-jet lag way and my head feels full and slow. On my way back along the highway I see bright primary colours. In a background of white and sand they stick out. It's a life-sized Homer Simpson, next to him his friend Barney, and next to that their good pal Spider-man. They're all surrounding a bar. Of course, I go in. The midday sun is punching through onto the terrace between giant windboards all painted brightly with graffiti. I didn't realise how hot the sun actually was until now in the cool shade. Being working-class English means I'm still incredibly uncomfortable with table service, so to shortcut the whole thing I walk into the back of the bar. I walk past a large man in a white vest and pencil moustache who is daring me to notice he's a stereotype. The bright colours stop at the terrace, along with the furniture and hygiene. The waitress speaks no English, so the first part of the exchange is taken up with her explaining how I should have sat down and had table service - a process made a little tougher than it should by her insistence in looking over to the other waitress and laughing. I sit back on the terrace where the music is just loud enough to drown out the traffic and the breeze feels as good as the cold breakfast beer. A man arrives with a keyboard under his arm so big Rick Wakeman would have turned it down as "a bit much". Being the only audience member of a giant keyboard serenade isn't going to make this day better, so I get up to leave. As I stand up and finish my beer the napkin sticks to the bottle then somehow sticks to my shirt when I put the bottle down. As I look up, I see the two waitresses laughing again with Mexican Rick at the English guy who apparently tucks a napkin into his shirt like a bib to enjoy a beer. I stuff the napkin in my pocket and leave.

Later, while emptying my pockets to get into the hammock on the hostel's roof I find the napkin. On it is an advertisement for La Isla Shopping Centre. It's a mall over on the archipelago of developed hotels and resort complexes - normally the sum total of what people see when they visit Cancún. I've never been on a hammock before but it turns out the combination of this stupid cold I've picked up and the constant movement means I'm asleep in minutes. I'm a natural.

****

"Have you been to Cancún before?" asks the taxi driver with only a little accent. The taxi is comfortable, too comfortable. The seats in the back feel like a mattress, they're reclined and the windows are tinted a deep blue. It's more like an isolation tank than a taxi. I have to sit up to talk.

"No, first time," I say

"This is all fake." He says this with pride as he gestures to the hotels over to one side,. "Built up by the government." We get to a stretch of road with water on each side. "Do you know what that is?" he says, pointing to the water on the left.

"The sea?" I ask. His rear-view mirror has two tiny pink Adidas trainers hanging from them.

"Good!" he says, "And this?" He points to the other side.

"More sea?" I say. He gives a little chuckle

"It's a lagoon," he says "You know the difference?" I tell him I don't. "Crocodiles," he says with pride. "Don't mix them up". He drops me off outside of the 'shopping village' which, anyway you cut it, is a mall. A large sterile mall, empty and jarringly aspatial. It could be anywhere - cool marble walls and slick shopping outlets, the only thing reminding you you're in Mexico is the tat in the gift shops and the giant replica of the Mayan calendar on the traffic island outside. It was a mistake to come here. Death would never be allowed here, even if there are crocodiles. My head is pounding and my bones are heavy.

Don't you dare judge me, but I find myself in Hooters. For four reasons: firstly, my cold needs hot wings to clear my sinuses; secondly, Hooters was the only restaurant without people outside hassling you to come in, which I was actually grateful for. The other two reasons belong to Luisa who has kindly put up with me changing my given table until I could find a seat with my back against a wall. Okay, so Hooters is vulgar, crass, and morally questionable, but so am I. There's a family at the next table, all wearing matching sun visors and generic basketball vests, except the daughter who has a straw hat and white vest top. The mom has a giant tattoo of a gun and a rose that takes up her entire upper arm. They're all wearing an all-inclusive resort bracelet with tan lines behind them. They're getting up to leave as my wings arrive.

"It's good to get out, see outside for a change," says the dad as they make their way out.

****

That night I go for a walk. The heat gets oppressive and, despite being ill, sitting felt like stewing in my own sweat. I don't know where I'm heading. I just pick a direction and walk. For the most part it seems to be along a four-lane highway. The surroundings get more and more urban, less polished, cracks in the concrete, broken glass embedded on top of the walls. Every time I look ahead there seems to be some neon or a bright sign that something is just ahead, but every time I get there it'll be a closed car showroom or mattress outlet store. Then sure enough, just ahead, another flickering promise, a fluorescent mirage I can't help shuffle towards with the same road-worn hope, grateful for the distraction.

****

All of the bunks at the hostel have a mini fan attached to the bed frame. Last night the clip must have come loose because I wake feeling a pulsing close to my face, and when I open my eyes I see the blades whirring inches away. This is terrifying, but the jolt that I need to drag my sore meat sack out of bed and outside of the hostel to meet my ride. Today, ill or not, I'm going to see one of the Seven Wonders of the World.

Julio is behind the counter this morning. I can hear the commentary and, if I angle my head, I can see a small television showing a soccer match. By the tone and excitement in the commentators' voices this must be an important match.

"Danny, you're up early," says Julio, friendly for someone at the arse-end of an all-night shift.

"I've got that tour today, said it'll pick me up at eight," I remind Julio, who I booked the tour with yesterday. I made sure it was him because I know they get a commission. He looks at the clock.

"So you're up here now?"

"It's five to eight," I say, confused.

"Suuuuure," he says. "Don't stand in the sun."

At half past eight, when I'm still outside, I realise why Julio reacted like that and, at a quarter to nine, just before I was about to go back inside and ask Julio to call the tour operators, a blue people carrier turns up.

There's no-one in it, apart from the driver. Said driver is a huge guy, big enough for me to forget about the inconvenience and all intentions I had about mentioning how long I've been waiting. As I get into the van, U2 play on the stereo and I hum along to 'I Still Haven't Found What I'm Looking For'. It's a bit on the nose but does remind me that I'm on a quest. Then we head off, in what I'm pretty sure is, the opposite direction.

I recognise the road. We're back on the road for Hotel Zone. Once you get past the cluster of bars at the top, everything we drive past is a hotel or a building site which will be a hotel very soon. Hotel or Soon-Hotel seem to be the only states in which space can exist in the Hotel Zone. You can tell how fancy a hotel is by its proximity to the road. Expensive hotels will be behind a fence with a driveway and grounds. The busier, less upmarket, places will have reception in sight of the road.

By now we've picked up a few more people and we're dropped at a place between hotels on the strip. The box office is right on the road and I have to remind myself to reject the snobbishness of the judgement I seem to have absorbed on the drive over. The building is a giant hut. The thatched roof is ludicrously high and everything about it feels like a theme park, including the queues. To the right is a box office with three windows, there are lines from two of them. There seems to be some confusion about which window to go to, so I head to the empty one and hand them all the tickets and forms I filled out yesterday with Julio. The woman smiles, takes one small ticket from the middle of the pile, rips off a corner and gives me a gold wristband. I'm not normally impressed by this sort of thing. I only remember it because there is a loud red-faced German guy angrily explaining that he should have the gold wristband, not the blue. The woman is waiting for security to come and simply stating - in much better and more polite English - that he paid for the blue one and the only difference is the gold wristband gets breakfast. "Ooo breakfast," I think.

I don't really know what is included in the trip. The day before, in a fugue of illness and sun boiled brain, I hastily bought the ticket because today, I realised, is the winter equinox, and I'd read somewhere that it is a special day to visit the ruins of Chichen Itza.

Chichen Itza was built around 550AD by the Mayans. The Mayans were generally a peace-loving farming bunch who invented a system of mathematics, including the concept of zero - something the Greeks had not bothered with - and an incredibly accurate method of astronomy. Chichen Itza was the centre of this society till around 800BC when they abandoned it for reasons they didn't record anywhere. Around 1000AD the Toltecs, a conquering Aztec force, took the city and turned it once again into a city state, bringing with them the warrior caste and their gods. In 2007 it was named one of the Seven Wonders of the World and is now one of the most visited historical sites in Mexico.

Inside the cabana still feels fake. The walls are concrete with a brick pattern scored into them, the bamboo wall of the gift shop has a glass automatic door seamlessly embedded into it. I walk into an area with a table set aside for food. Immediately the waiter appears and asks if I would like orange juice or coffee. I ask for tea - my colonial instincts are apparently hard to hide. I'm then asked if I want the American or the Mexican breakfast.

Honestly, I want neither but ask for the Mexican one because fuck it, I was curious and I've got a gold wristband.

Mexican breakfast turns out to be some sort of omelette served with refried beans and a salad. One of the Australians on the table next to me wonders out loud

"Is this what Mexicans have for breakfast?"

"It is if they come here," I say with a shrug. The Australian looks confused. He got the joke, it's just I'm fifteen years older than him, making dad jokes, and expecting the room to crack up.

Seemingly without any signal everyone with the same wristband as me gets up and heads towards the gift shop exit. As we leave, the German guy is getting redder, his tattoos melding into his veiny arms, as he tries to insist "Zey are blue!"

The buses are through a park with high fences and a winding path, like a maze. Around every corner is a pressed concrete statue or relief of Mayan or Atzec culture. I realise this is a queuing system and we're going through the wrong way. The giant hut is the entrance to an adventure activity centre with a Mayan theme. A literal theme park.

The car park is shared with the golf club next door. As we pull out, I can see the course: the deepest most unnatural green colour, with flats and dips that have nothing to do with the landscape that surrounds them. As a true child of the eighties - one that cut his intellectual teeth during the height of postmodernism - I'm really not fussed by notions of the authentic or unnatural, but the landscape and the artifice so far is disquieting, like trespassing into someone else's idea of beauty.

****

Our tour guide, Martine, is a tall man with a deep colouring and who looks more Native American than Spanish. He takes the mic naturally and his first order of business is to count how many people speak English and how many speak Spanish. He does this alternating each block of speech between the two languages. The split is about half.

"Well the tour is sold as English but with the amount of Spanish speakers I will have to do both, so what I'm going to do is speak Spanish first and then English so I don't have to keep switching each sentence and speak Spanglish." Half the coach laughs. "So what I'm going to ask is that the English speakers have a little patience and trust I'm not saying bad things about you." Now the other half laughs. His manner at this point is gameshow host charming -, likable until you decide it's not. I had decided it was not.

Martine then launches into a spiel in Spanish, that, from its rhythms, delivery, and the way half the coach laughs, is very similar to a stand-up routine. This goes on for an hour and a half in Spanish - yes, I've timed it. English time, he talks about the Mayan village we are about to visit, how authentic the people are, and how poor they are and how we should consider spending our money there. After all, they themselves are just pursuing "the American dream". He also underlines the ancient

Mayan wisdom and passes around slips of paper for us to write down our date of birth in case we want to buy our "personalised Mayan horoscope," presented on "real papyrus". The sell is unusually hard, at one point referencing "Americans" who usually stay "ignorant" to "ancient teachings". And for 500 pesos it's not cheap. None of this has the rhythm of his earlier speech in Spanish and takes less than half an hour to deliver.

As we get closer to our first stop he reminds us all we should have bought "jungle strength" insect repellent with us because we are so far inland and the insects are more dangerous and could make us "really sick". The normal repellent we might have bought back home wouldn't be strong enough. Luckily, he is selling high-strength insect repellent on the bus in case we didn't have it. He adds that he's now not legally responsible if one of us gets sick.

After one last warning to be "open minded and respectful" we debark the coach. The driver is waiting by the door and, as everybody gets off, he asks us to stand still while he takes a photograph. Martine tells us this is for a "surprise". We are led solemnly through a wooded area to a shaman wearing a headdress and loincloth. His body has been painted with red and black stripes and his deep craggy face is half painted red. He is attended by a younger man wearing immaculate white linen clothes and a red head scarf. There are bundles of sage burning. We all gather in front of him and quietly wait for what's next. Martine explains we are about to be blessed as a group and, for a small gratuity, we can be blessed individually afterwards.

The priest reaches for the sage and begins his blessing in the most high-pitched voice I have ever heard an adult human use, ever. My eyes widen with suppressed laughter and Martine glowers at us.

After our blessing, the presentation turns to the subject of obsidian and, as Martine kindly translates, we are taught of the healing, cleansing and focusing uses of the black stone. Martine tells us he regularly visits this shaman with his autistic son and that the shaman's squeaky chant "activates the ions" in this magical stone and now his son can speak. Presumedly to say "Can we please not visit the semi-naked man who screams at us in dolphin anymore dad?".

We are then led to a hut filled with obsidian jewellery and knick-knacks for sale. Manned by three or four attendants, they take cash and card. We are left to browse for half an hour. Some people bought stuff out of boredom. We were there long enough for me to notice the cameras installed in the room and supporting walls of the hut.

After a painfully long time we are led to the entrance of a cave, ducking down onto the wooden platform built around the blue green rocks. I take a breath of cool, crisp air, suddenly noticing the sun's relentless burn and the weird wet warmth of the climate by its absence. The stairs lead to a pool of turquoise water, somehow serene and still despite the tourists splashing around in it. Cenotes are underground fresh-water caves that were the only source of drinking water for the Maya and were treated with the mythic respect reserved for something that keeps you alive. The atmosphere is holy, a place that deserves reverence. I sit on the edge of the platform and look deep into the cave, the water is glass clear and goes from turquoise and green to black as the depths go beyond light. The Maya believed cenotes to be the entrance to the underworld. At these holy sites they would throw people in to keep the balance and appease the gods that dwelt there. If the person survived their words were treated as prophecy. Death isn't here. If he is, he's at the bottom of that pool silent and waiting.

Back on the coach, I'm hurting. The illness has started to make me sore, and the bits that were already sore downright hurt. Quickly I'm asleep.

I'm woken by somebody handing me something. I look at it, it's a plastic shot glass. Tuning into Martine on the mic he's explaining it's a Mayan liqueur. One of the Mayan people from the village is on the coach with us, he gives a toast and we all down the shot. It's ansiseedy with honey notes, reminds me of a bitter mead. Martine tells us there are bottles for sale. I'm handed a bottle of yellowish clear liquid with my face on the label. It's not a weird dream, I recognise the photo as the one the driver took as we got off the coach. The booze is about £15 and if they wanted me to buy it, if they knew me at all they would have kept my picture off it.

We are hustled off the coach and given one last warning by Martine not to buy the "useless junk" from the vendors. He has the nerve to do this with a straight face. The coach group is split between those who want the tour in Spanish who are taken by Martine, and the remainder of us who are given to Pedro.

Pedro is a chestnut brown man in his fifties, with a rangy build and short cropped hair. He's dressed in board shorts and a long sleeve Billabong top, looking nothing like the other tour guides in various states of uniforms and lanyards and badges. When Pedro speaks his voice is a deep, West Coast American accent except when he pronounces Spanish flawlessly. Pedro has a calmness to him - a comfortable quiet. He explains he recently got his ancestry tested and is 60% Native American, 30% Spanish European and 10% Irish English. He tells us this because, as he explains, the Mayans native to the area tend to be 100% Mayan. This means that as well as being below average height, they don't sweat, have any body hair, rarely go bald or recede, and stay incredibly active into old age.

His attitude to the vendors selling "illegal" merchandise is a bit more even. He tells us that the cheap Chinese-made merch devalues the true crafts and products produced in Mexico, but tempers it with the knowledge a lot of people's livelihoods depend on it. When someone asks if they should buy off these vendors he gives a little shrug "that's up to you".

As we walk around the site, Pedro tells us of a vast bustling city where the Maya and Telocs ruled side-by-side, and where people would travel for months to come and sell their wares. The locals were taxed but, because money wasn't often used, the tax would take the form of the first batch of whatever was produced. By this time we've reached a place Pedro called the War Palace, essentially the base of military power: "the Toltec Pentagon".

"Are any of you the first-born child?" he asks, I raise my hand, no one else does. His face gestures a small surprise. "Okay, so what I was saying about taxes, well that went for children too," he's talking to me directly.

"You would have been taken from your parents at around seven and given training to be a warrior." he reaches out and puts a hand on my shoulder "First couple of years would have been spent toughening you up, giving you physically hard work and not much food. Then they would spend a couple of years conditioning you, training you not to fear death," he looks directly at me, "Wouldn't that be nice, not to fear death?"

He refers back to this warrior's journey throughout the rest of the tour - describing the festivals I would have attended, the sacrifices I would have seen, and the sports I would have played - until we get to the main temple, the four-sided pyramid known as El Castillo. Pedro tells us it is a temple to the feathered snake god, Kukulcan. Each side of the temple faces one of the cardinal compass directions and each face has 91 stairs, which, when you include the step at the top, add up to 365, the number of days in a solar year. The room on top is an acoustic box that amplifies sound. Pedro claps and encourages us to do the same, when we do the temple emits an echoey tribbing sound. Pedro finishes the tour and we take turns to slip him some pesos, which he accepts discreetly before disappearing.

Behind the temple the sky is black with clouds and the winds are whipping through the crowd of 300 or so people waiting for the equinox. The temple is arranged in such a way that, during the few days either side of both the summer and winter equinox, the sun hits the steps on one corner of the temple and the shadow makes an undulating snake that appears to crawl down the temple stairs and join the stone serpent's head that decorates the end.

Occasionally the clouds break and we see the beginning of the snake form. At other times the sky darkens even more and we are promised some other sort of show. The crowd thickens. There's a woman at the front wearing a traditional white tunic embroidered with flowers, her thick black hair braided with matching flowers. She is swaying in time with the four or five people sitting around her, clapping and shaking instruments. Every time the clouds cover the sun she deflates and blows into an object she keeps in her cupped hand.

The clouds thicken over the sun in a more permanent way and I see her shoulders sag, but she doesn't sit down or leave. I do. I leave her there waiting for a glimpse of divinity, for a blessing that may never come.

Back on the coach the energy is low. The heat is radiating off the pre-sunburnt - but insect bite free - skin of the rest of the coach. A little while into the journey, Martine, presumably with nothing more to sell, announces there is beer available for those that want it. The coach driver's assistant - a boy of about 15 - hands out the plastic cups

"You want cerveza?" he asks as he gets to me.

"Yes please," I say.

"You're English?" he says, figuring it out either by my accent or enthusiasm.

"Yes I am," I say. He hands me two of the plastic cups.

At this point most of the coach is asleep, and those that are left are not big beer drinkers because my cup keeps getting refreshed. It's hard to tell if I'm getting drunk.

I'm definitely getting numb. This should be a good time but I'm on my own. I'm lonely, I realise. I examine the feeling because I don't think I get lonely often but, surprisingly, I know the feeling and it's familiar, too familiar.

Four years ago both my best friends, independently of each other, moved away. I'm fine, I told myself, I'm a lone wolf. A ronin. I keep my own council. But this was a low ebb dragging at my subconscious. I've been lonely for four years and only just realised. Is this why She broke up with me? Oh God, She's been my only friend for four years and I'm insufferable. That's a lot to take on by yourself. That wasn't fair on Her at all.

My cups are filled again and the boy leaves the rest of the bottle as well.

I must tell her. I take out my phone and text her this revelation, apologising for putting her through that. It's about four in the morning but she'll read it when she wakes up. I hit send. About 10 minutes later I get a confused "okay thanks" back. She obviously doesn't get it. I'll text her one more time to clarify what I meant.

No, don't do that. Drunk Autopilot kicks in. He's a nice guy, always three drinks behind how drunk I currently am, Sitting in my head keeping me safe, but a bit of a killjoy. I can't help but resent this voice even though it has saved my life a couple of times.

In fact, let's delete that text. Maybe it never happened, and if it did you won't be able to read it in the morning and explode with shame. I do what he says, the tendrils of regret snake at my skin. No, don't think about that now. Do a sleep instead.

Already my arms and back are burning. The panic is like stomach acid. I keep swallowing it down. I dig in. I keep expecting the waves I feel swelling behind me to push me towards the beach. Each time I rise with them but am left behind. I'm not moving. Soon I won't be able to swim anymore.

3. Dead Famous

Full bone-chill has taken over. I'm sweating, but sweating in the different way you do when it's just heat. A clammy ectoplasm of ill that drenches you. My nose is alternating between streaming freely and blocked. I try to remember yesterday, I'm getting flashes of a helium shaman and an apocalyptic sky. I get pain in my chest. Did I speak to Her? I remember I texted. I check my phone and just her answer is there. I remember Drunk Autopilot telling me I wouldn't want to remember and I take his word for it.

"Un boleto a Mérida por favor." I'm reading off a piece of paper at the bus station. The lady behind the counter laughs and gives a little clap to my clearly expectant face. I smile. By now whatever cold I have, the hangover, and my acidic regret have combined into one malevolent entity I have named 'El Bastard' which is making it hard to do anything other than push my face on the cool tiled floor and sob convincingly.

"Es muy español buen?" I ask. She is smiling with an edge of wince now. She makes the 'so-so' motion with her hand and laughs at my pantomimed disappointment. At my senior school, each year took French or Spanish alternately. My year was a French year - I dropped the subject so I could do both Drama and Art. My French teacher was furious because she thought I was great at French but all I did was frankenstein some elaborate sentences together from the vocab books, then picked up on the context clues for any reply. The

Spanish I do know has been picked up from TV and movies so any sense I can make really is a win for me.

I conduct the rest of the purchase in what I hope are charming hand gestures. I honestly thought I was 10 years past my 'cute but bumbling foreigner' routine, but there we are. The last time I used it was in India and that didn't quite go as planned.

****

I find the enquiries desk and ask where I can buy a new ticket. They take the ticket off me, almost throw it back, and point to the train about to pull away from the platform. I swing my rucksack onto one shoulder and run for the train with less than a minute to spare.

"What car is this?" I ask the guy next to me. He's wearing a bobble hat and heavy jacket on a humid night.

"S14," he says. "What car do you want on your ticket?" I look at my ticket.

"S3," I say. He chuckles.

"S3 very far away that way, after upper class."

Now, this means not only do I have to carry my rucksack through at least 11 carriages, but I have to carry it in front of me so I can maneuver it through the gaps and over obstacles down the narrow walkways. Not something I relish. My plan was this: hang around the end bit of this carriage until the next stop then alight, run down the platform and get back on at the right carriage.

Pros: (i) avoid the English-cringe inducing 'excuse me-sorry' mumbleathon; (ii) not having to do the hardest arm workout since I stopped going to the gym over Christmas because I was sad.

Cons: (i) unspecified wait outside train toilet; (ii) if I fuck up I'm trapped in the middle of nowhere.

Seeing as there was nowhere that I really had to be, and I was covered in monkey piss anyway, I decide it's too late to be fussy. But the decision is out of my hands: a ticket inspector asks for my ticket and sends me on my way down the train.

I get about four carriages (that's 37 'excuse mes' and 'sincerely sorrys' in English money) before I have to stop. While getting my breath back a studenty looking chap asks me, "Do you not have a seat number?" He wears thin-framed glasses and has a circular scar under his eye. I explain my story and he laughs. "Of course the train is full, there is a Krishna festival in Jaipur, most people are going."

"It's just that I feel bad for bumping all these people after they've settled in," I say. His English is great and it's good not to have to speak with the simpler grammar I've been favouring.

"Oh, people don't mind, it happens on Indian trains anyway." He reaches over and rubs my head. "Your hair is blue! Krishna was Blue!"

I heave my bag through eight more carriages. The train then stops. I know two things: (i) even if it's just stopped on the sidings to let people off I'm also getting off and going for it; and (ii) if it pulls away without me I'm turbo-buggered. People spill out. It's a platform so I swing my bag and push through the crowds. I see S3, yes! I try the door, locked. Buggerbuggerbugger. I run to the other end and try the door - locked again. BUGGERBUGGER-BUGGER. The whistle blows, TUUURBO BUGGER. I try the next door, it opens and I push in. My heart is still beating when I find my bunk empty.

And with one last heave of aching arms I stuff my bag on and curl around it.

****

Buoyed by my interaction with the ticket lady I decide El Bastard can be kept at bay by food and distraction, so I wander around looking for something to eat. I end up on a tourist strip, where all the restaurants seem to think the best way of attracting patrons is by playing incredibly loud European house music or by painting themselves in McDonalds colours and having beer glasses on their logo. La Parrilla is decked out in a tasteful terracotta and has an awning, which I think is fancy.

The inside is white and terracotta with solid wooden furniture with a vomit of decoration on all the walls: flags, folk art, fresco, all in garish colours. El Bastard stirs. The waiter comes over and I order a beer. He brings it over, he gives me the bottle and then gestures. I ignore it and drink the beer, but I can see out of the corner of my eyes he's tying his shoes. I take another pull of the beer and notice he's been down there a long time. I look over and he's crouched next to me with a glass balanced on his head. I realise the gesture he made was for me to pour the beer into the glass. He's making eye contact, making it somehow my fault I've messed up a perfectly normal head pouring beer interaction. I finish the bottle looking at him and meekly ask for another. He leaves in a huff.

I never normally order a starter but I realise it's been a day or so since I've eaten, so I order some nachos before the burrito comes out. The nachos land at the table almost immediately and I attack them heartily. While I'm doing this a bigger, more robust plate of nachos arrive and I realise the first nachos were not my starter nachos - they were pre-nacho nachos. Now my real nachos are here and I'm not as hungry. I order another beer. When the burrito arrives it comes with a side order of nachos and I want to throw them at the mariachi band that started a few minutes into my post pre-nacho nachos. El Bastard is telling me all the waiters think I'm a fun-ruining, nacho-obsessed gringo and I should leave. I can see them in my head looking over.

"He hates fun.'

"Did you try the head pour trick?"

"Yes he hated it."

"He's looking at the mariachi funny."

"Let's put glass in his dessert, he's clearly not La Parrilla material."

I pay with a big tip and leave, trying to look like I'm enjoying the Mexican folk song the band play, while they focus on the big table of punters who are clearly more La Parrilla material than me.

****

The next day I've time to kill before my bus. I go for a wander. El Bastard has moved on and I want to be amongst people without a malevolent force whispering in my head. Sundays in Cancún, it appears, are much like Sundays in England, except warmer and with less Antiques Roadshow. Everything is closed as I make my way to the main square, and the odd person I do see seems dazed.

In downtown Cancún the local shop fronts have nowhere near the level of polish, so the big brands stick out here. Everything seems to be in a state of rebuilding or slow decay, but I guess that describes everything in the world, ever.

The central square is bright and airy, and looks brand new. A kids play area is in one corner, flanked on one side by permanent food counters with mobile food stalls around the perimeter. The food counter area has seating which is populated by families watching their kids in the play area, or in one of the tiny electric cars available to hire and drive around in front of the main stage in the middle of the square, which, at the moment is playing mariachi music for seemingly no one but the pitched, Mad-Max style face-off going on.

At the back of the square I see a sign for one-dollar margaritas. The bar is right on the street with fixed bar stools under the shade of a tree that makes up the corner of the building. I pitch up and order what turns out to be the worst margarita in Mexico. It tastes of watery regret and tequila's shadow.

I finish it as fast as I can, which I think the bartender mistakes for enthusiasm.

"Otro, another?" he asks.

I involuntarily make a face and say "Corona por favor."

The bartender understands with a shrug.

Everywhere is dressed for a fiesta. Paper decorations in red, yellow and white, and the sort of foil decorations my parents would hang everywhere for Christmas, mismatched dangling from a ceiling where. Every so often, the music stops and someone checks the mics in the universal language of 'Roadie'.

"Uno, dos, uno dos tres."

Not that the other patrons notice, they're enthralled at the nil - nil draw happening on the monitors. I let out a sigh and realise I'm happy. It's a feeling as foreign as the commentary coming from the TV, but I am and I resolve to enjoy it for as long as it lasts.

Someone else comes to the bar and orders the margarita. He takes a sip and orders a beer. I meet the barman's eye, we both smile and he gives a 'can't win them all' shrug. While the bar is watching the football I'm watching the tiny electric cars. One girl is in a replica Mercedes but is driving it sitting backwards, steering with her back pressed against the steering wheel, flooring it wildly with her hands. As I watch, she mounts the barrier and is rescued by two adults rushing over, clearly more concerned about the car. The look on her face tells me it wasn't an accident.

The commentators of the football match are reaching a crescendo and it's enough for me to pay attention to the screen. It's just a corner and, in the words of The Who, I won't get fooled again. The commentators are now screaming at what appears to be a simple substitution. Mexican football players are broader than Premier

League players, kinder eyes as well.

What I took for the end of the day seems to be the beginning of the evening. More stalls are being set-up and every so often a tiny Mexican pushing an impossibly big stall will chunder past and begin prepping. I can see one woman on a stall chopping peppers with her hands but using her foot to rock a baby in a car seat underneath. I've forgotten how many beers I've had at this point and I'm finding myself short of breath because my nose is still blocked. A Mexican version of 'Yes Sir, I Can Boogie' is on the main stage speakers, it's better in Spanish.

An American family walks past. The dad asks the group "Do we want one here?" The rest of the party's eyes glide across the bar, and me. No, no-one thinks we should have one here. Maybe they heard about the margaritas, or maybe it was the guy opposite me that hawked up a wad of phlegm and spat it onto the floor next to him? The bartender saw it happen but didn't say a word. Just another evening.

The bartender's T-shirt boasts this place has the best shrimp in Cancún (according to Tripadvisor). I was going to leave but he took my staring at his T-shirt as a request for another beer, so I guess I'm stuck. The sky is almost entirely a navy-blue cloud, but the heat is unflinchingly present. No one seems bothered. It's thunderstorm weather and no-one has a coat.

I look around for the instructor, he's not around. I never considered how lonely dying would be. The last ever person I ever spoke to and I doubt whether he remembers my name.

4. The Road Death Travelled

With tinted windows and strips of blue neon, the coach I'm in feels like it's the middle of the night. Specifically, the middle of the night in Tokyo in 2050. To add to the cyberpunk aesthetic, every four seats a screen hangs from the overhead compartments. It's three hours or so to Merida and I'm engrossed in a documentary which I think is about the cultural significance of fish and chips. It's hard to tell because it's entirely in Spanish. Luckily there are subtitles. Unfortunately these are also in Spanish.

I'm so engrossed I don't notice we've been stopped on the highway. I glance out of my window and see a checkpoint with four men dressed in light blue uniforms, somewhere halfway between public servant and military fatigues. Each one carries a large, black, automatic weapon. The surliest of these men gets on and says something to the coach party. I don't know what he says but people are reaching for things, slowly. I get my ticket and passport out from the sweaty body wallet under my T-shirt.

The police guard makes his way down the bus looking at the passengers but not checking their documentation. He gets to me and stops, I hand him my ticket and passport. I'm nervous that he still has one hand casually on the very big gun. The gun is frightening. It is matte black with tiny nicks and bumps. It's scary because of its lack of glamour: it's an object, a tool, functional and everyday. I'm lost staring at the gun, wondering if it's ever killed anyone - I know guns don't kill people, bullets do. Bullets fired from big fucking guns like the one I'm staring at, wielded by people like this guy scowling at me. He's looking at my bus ticket, the disdain on his face making it very clear that he is not a ticket inspector. He takes my passport and looks at it really hard, then hands it back and leaves the coach. Mine is the only ID he's checked.

The rest of the journey is taken up with playing out all the possible scenarios and, compared to what was going on in my head, I got off lightly. In one scenario he asks what I'm doing in Mexico and I answer honestly:

"A slow-motion nervous breakdown," Or even,

"I'm looking for Death, do you know him?"

"So why are you going to Merida?" he asks.

"Because it's the site of one of his greatest hits," I explain.

"Merida?"

"Well, yes, near there anyway. Single deaths, multi-car pile-ups, spree killers, natural disasters; all pale in comparison to a mass extinction event."

Later I'm dragged off the coach in handcuffs, shouting "It's fine, I'm a writer not a lunatic. The distinction is fine but it's there."

"It's there," I sob, as I'm stuffed into the back of a police van.

****

Meanwhile, 65 million years ago, the swamp was hot and, well, swampy. An alligator slowly rises, first, its cold eyes, then snout, followed by a slow reveal of its stone-like hide. It's a slow day in the swamp. The alligator doesn't know it, but it's Thursday. Its eyes, attracted to movement, scan the brackish water and then the trees, and then slowly it raises them to the sky. The sky has a thing it's never seen before - a large red and black blot. It doesn't seem to be moving, but it is getting bigger.

"Bollocks," thinks the alligator as it sinks to the bottom of the swamp, where it stays, waiting.

****

The heat hits me as soon as I get off the coach. Having looked at maps of Merida on the coach, I thought I had it cracked. It's a grid system numbered 1–100: the odd numbers going east to west and even numbers going north to south. But the heat has other plans. Despite being confident about my route to the hostel 30 seconds before, as I set out of the coach station it all falls to shit under the relentless noon sun. Everything but my lizard brain has shut down. The 15-minute walk is stretching into a 45-minute SAS induction yomp and trying to work out the numbering system has become like trying to solve a five-dimensional Rubik's cube. I walk in three large circles around streets with near-identical, boxy, one-story buildings and arrive at the same launderette twice, before realising the map I have is using colours as well numbers. The laundrette is 'Blue 12', my hostel is 'Green 12'. I'm a genius.

In a dehydrated daze I check into the hostel and, after drinking all the water, change into my shorts and head straight to the pool. It's surrounded by tall tropical trees and stone walls. Hammocks are suspended over the pool by a dark brown wooden structure and are just high enough to let your foot dangle into turquoise water. It's hot still, but overcast. I swing side-to-side, allowing my English body to acclimatise. There are two Israeli girls loudly having 'The backpacker conversation'. When the 'everything-has-an-energy' and 'the-universe-is-obviously-teaching-me-something' has become too much, I roll out of the hammock, not bothering to take off my shirt or sunglasses, and sink to the bottom of the pool, allowing the sweet nothing of the water crowd out the banal oppressive air.

Floating. Holding my breath. I can feel the pressure all around me but as long as I don't open my eyes I'll be okay. For the last 10 years, on and off, I've been working with young people that don't fit anywhere else. Special Educational Needs, Emotional Behavioural Disorders, and all shades of the Autistic Spectrum. My last job was at a special school which I loved, but one day they took me to one side. Apparently they needed my 'size, weight, power' in another classroom - the classroom with the most profound needs. The days then alternated between crippling boredom and intense situations that require hands on interaction. As a worker with young people, putting your hands on is a last resort; a decision not to be taken lightly that has the potential to destroy any relationship you've built with that young person. It's physically and emotionally draining and happens in this classroom nearly every day. I go from loving my job to hating it. This is what it felt like: pressure, numbness. I close my eyes and just get through the next minute, 10 minutes, few days, weeks, the next term. In this numb cocoon, this foetal sack of self-preservation and denial, I simply didn't notice that She had slipped away, too someone else, someone present I push up and gasp for air.

The next day I'm at reception trying to arrange a taxi.

"Where do you want to go?" says the distracted woman behind the counter.

I hand her a piece of paper with the name written on it, rather than butcher it with my clumsy English mouth.

"Chicxulub?" she asks.

"If that's how you pronounce that, yes" I say.

"Why?" she asks.

I'm not prepared for this. I try to think of the easiest way of explaining that 65 million years ago a 10-15 km asteroid hit Earth in that spot causing the death of 75% of species on the planet, let alone that I'm looking for the anthropomorphic personification of Death, and I think starting with his greatest hits might be a good start.

"Sightseeing," I say.

"But there's nothing there," she's adamant.

I really don't know why she's playing gatekeeper. She's one of the pretty Israeli girls from the pool yesterday. I'm the guy that 'fell' out of the hammock into the pool with all his clothes on.

"I could ask in town?" I say. She sees I'm serious.

"No, that's okay, I will tell the driver you need him to wait," she says. "If you wait by the pool I'll tell you when they are here."

The taxi is surprisingly new and comfortable. The driver is not quite middle age and, when we agree to a price, he turns the meter off. He doesn't seem to be chatty, which is a relief. I wonder if the questions you ask a taxi driver are a global phenomenon or intrinsically British, but I don't have the Spanish for "been busy mate? What time do you finish your shift?" Let alone "Do people ask you if you've been busy a lot?". The city of Merida melts away quickly. In minutes we're on a highway driving through green desert, scrubland, and every so often a white stone wall or part of a building can be seen. Going past at speed it's hard to tell if it's in the process of construction or decay. We have turned, perhaps, two corners since the city. After that we've just followed the telephone pylons. We pass a couple of gas stations and eventually the buildings start becoming more finished and more frequent. And before I know it we've pulled up beside a large adobe church in what, I suppose, is a town square. The grass is a vibrant green next to a bandstand. Over the road is a sports pitch with a stand at the far end. It's sedate, nothing seems open and the few people that are about seem to have places to go.

I go for a walk to find a cantina or shop, and I settle for one of the million Oxo convenience stores that populate every other shopfront in the bigger towns. There is nothing, but not the sort of nothing that would be left after the asteroid hit. I try to imagine the impact of 420 zettajoules of energy that would trigger a global firestorm. I look into the distance expecting to be in a valley, but it all looks flat to me. It's clean here, idyllic. More like heaven than the blackened hell pit equivalent of a nuclear winter. I go for a walk and end up back at the taxi.

Driving back, I can't help but feel small. Less than small. I expected more. If not physical evidence, some sort of psychic scar - a mood, something. If a global catastrophe with the energy equivalent of a billion Hiroshima's can disappear leaving evidence only trained geologists can spot, then what is one life? Any life? A hundred lives? We're just the microbes crawling on the face of God. I think I'm crying. The air conditioning dries the tears as quickly as they form. The taxi driver makes eye contact in the mirror, he turns the radio down.

"Are you okay?" he asks, genuinely concerned.

"Yeah," I say wiping my face. "Been busy today?"

****

The sky has become ominous by the time I'm changed and out, walking the cobbled roads of Merida. The buildings are built in what I suppose you'd call a colonial style: the same flourishes and styles you see in some of the towns in Goa. The Europeans got around. Merida is known as 'The White City' although the houses are painted all the pastel hues. The colours fading to greys in the dark sky which is thick with cloud. Even though it's not raining yet, flashes of lighting and rolls of thunder are making strangers look at each other for reassurance.

Illuminati Pizza is an open room with high ceilings and three sets of large barn doors, all of which are open. On one wall is a selection of illustrations and graphic art. I'm the only customer, so I order a couple of beers and a pizza. The place is slick and simple. The pizza is good and the beer is cold. Illuminati Pizza wouldn't be out of place in whichever borough of London is being gentrified at the moment. The pizza arrives at the same time as my third beer and, as it does, the sky finally rips. The ground outside sighs as sheets of water slam down. One of the waiters runs over to close the doors closest to me. I ask him, if it's okay, I'd rather watch the rain. He smiles, I think he would too.

I recognise this as one moment I'll keep, a sparkling shard of glass that won't get lost in the malaise of my memory. I'm crying for the second time today, but the tears need to be there as much as the ground needed the rain. The storm broke, and with it snapped something in me that needed to be broken.

****

The main square is busy and the traffic is far more metropolitan, despite everybody wandering in and out of it like it was a sleepy village. One side is dominated by the cathedral. I head in. It's dark and old wood. I can smell incense and my eyes are having a hard time adjusting to the dark. The space looks impossibly big. It looks like every old, European cathedral. Jarringly so, in the same way a McDonald's will look and work exactly the same, no matter where in the world you go. Catholicism did it first. Franchised salvation. It's hard not to have a sense of awe in a space so grand it kicks the crutches out of your head. Giant theatres designed to inspire a liminal state, a dissociation from outside the doors into a new way of being. Malleable, awed brains, seduced with eternal life and terrorised with eternal damnation.

I leave via the side door and wander for a while. As I'm dodging tourists with neckfulls of cameras and moms with pushchairs, I'm giddy with the notion that it's me who's the caricature, a pink haired anomaly. I push myself bodily into a doorway, trying to feel the solid wall as I hit it, to orientate myself in my own body and try to experience myself through my own senses, not what I'm projecting from other people's minds. I'm hot. The body wallet itches where it's stuck to my midriff. I'm thirsty, I notice the breeze over my feet. They're strangely light because they're not used to being out of the heavy boots I wear almost exclusively.

I'm in a square now, off the main drag. It's traditional yet polished and there is a giant loveseat for tourists to pose on. The love seat is two individual seats facing opposite ways, attached at the arms so the occupants can face each other if they turn sideways. It was to stop courting couples from getting too intimate under the ever-vigilant eye of their escort. I don't sit: even the thought of the empty seat across from me makes me hurt in a place I don't have anymore, like a phantom limb. The church on this square is Iglesia de Santa Lucía and is nowhere near as grand as the cathedral. Its smooth red walls lie back from the square and I only notice it's a church from the stained glass above the door.

Inside, the church is white and has small altars for the different saints along the walls There is a woman on the left praying to a figure of Christ, a wax model with the wounds of stigmata lying in a glass box. He's white, and his face is not dead but mournful. It's gory. Christanity is a death cult, it's the main selling point. There is no everlasting life but through me, says God. My only son died for you. Fear Death, love me.

The altar end is dominated by a giant frieze of a woman on a hillside talking to an angel. This is St Lucia herself. There is a small fire, that is mostly smoke, at the hem of her dress, a bowed oxen to the right hand bottom corner, and a man behind her about to strike her with a sword. According to the stories, St Lucia decided not to marry, pledged her virginity to God and her dowry to the poor. Her marriage was arranged anyway, though she tried to put her match off by removing her own eyes and delivering them to him. Her suitor reported her to the authorities. St Lucia's punishment was to be defiled in a brothel, but when they came to take her they found they couldn't move her, not even by dragging her with oxen. They tried to set her alight instead, but the fire wouldn't catch. Finally, she was stabbed in the throat by a sword. Later, when preparing her body for burial, they found her eyes were intact.

St Lucia is, among other things, the patron saint of authors. It seems right, although I can't put my finger on why. Probably the sheer bloody-mindedness. I put a few pesos in the collection tin and kneel down to light a candle. There's so much loss, so much I'm mourning for, that I can't choose and there are not enough candles for it all. I light a candle and say sorry to St Lucy herself. I pray the sword was quick and she wasn't too scared.

****

It's a widely accepted tactic when travelling to book a long journey for late in the evening so you travel overnight, not only saving money on accommodation for the night, but letting sleep take up a chunk of an otherwise boring coach/bus/train trip. As such, although checkout for most hostels is 10 in the morning, most of them will allow you to check out, but store your luggage and still use the facilities until you're due to go. So, I'm by the pool again, all packed and ready to travel. I ease into a hammock. There are a whole bunch of other travellers sunbathing and one guy is obnoxiously trying to pick up a couple of girls he's just met. I'm trying to ignore the patter; it's verging on the point of being creepy. His Americanisms are jarring with the accent and the persona swings wildly from crusty travel-ler-type to urban street-entrepreneur.

"Was 'spose to be out here a month, been gone three. Looking to make that cash, you know what I'm saying?"

One of the girls does know what he was saying but seems indifferent.

"We're all here just wanting to keep the party going," he adds.

I'm unsure of what he's pitching now, does he want sex, or a small business loan?

I'm shifting awkwardly, can't get comfy. I take off my body wallet and slip it into my bag. I take off my shirt, he is still going.

"Eating how the locals do, living like them. It's cheaper and more real." The girls are barely answering, his pitch is winding down and he's settled into the lounger next to them. I stick my earphones in.

I may have slept. I remember the rain coming later, but it's a relief, the pool empties and I'm left swinging in the hammock singing loudly to myself. The image of wax Jesus lying in his glass tomb seems to be my brain's screensaver. Gaudy, a reminder of not only the pain and torture of Jesus, but the viewers' fragile mortality. Christianity sought the monopoly of death, but it's dogma is exactly the thing that left gaps. Folklore fills the gaps left in dogma and so Death finds his job. The church says we have an afterlife, but does not specify how we get there. Maybe Death is just a taxi driver? Been busy mate? What time do you get off?

I can't swim anymore, I can barely move my arms or legs to stay afloat. The beach is exactly the same distance away as it was when I began swimming. I'm in trouble. I try to wave, in case anybody is on the shore, but I go under. Quickly I resurface, flailing. What was the thing they say about people drowning ? They go under three times before it's the last?

5. Death Is More

It's beginning to get dark by the time I get to the bus station and the atmosphere of tired frustration lends an edge to the place. The station itself is nice enough: halfway between medium airport and public bathroom in terms of white tile and wipe-clean plastic seats screwed into the floor. The fact they're never air-conditioned always throws me, they look air-conditioned in that municipal, mopped-floor, public space kind of way, but never are. They're actually massive, with doors that constantly open. It'd be insane to even try. But still, as you heave your rucksack through the doors it's always disappointing not to be hit by that fresh, slightly too crisp, air.

The people waiting are not smiling, but who smiles while waiting for a bus? I examine my discomfort and try to imagine how I'd feel if everybody here had white skin, and I would have felt safer. Now, this is an ugly thing to admit and I hope it has more to do with feeling more welcome around people like me than having negative feelings or associations towards other races.

There is a big guy with prison tattoos and angry muscles pacing by the door. My brain pleads its case - surely it's okay to be scared of him? That just seems like common sense. But then I catch a mom from a row of chairs over giving me the side eye and I mentally inventory my appearance: pink hair, piercings, visible tattoos, big chain, big black boots. I'm visually closer to him than her.

It's fairly late by the time the coach pulls off and despite the dubbed movies playing I fall asleep, rocked by the comforting feeling of my body moving through space. Coaches have been a fact of life for me since I was 17: too poor for trains (unless I'm hiding in the toilet), and too 'Me' to learn to drive. All my friends have, at some point, told me I should never learn to drive. Something about poor impulse control and low boredom threshold, I think. I may still be banned from even sitting in the front seat of a couple of people's cars. So it's been coaches. Luckily I'm a good passenger. I can sleep anytime, I don't get travel sick, I can read and write legibly and, even just sitting, I'm soothed by the sensation of my body hurtling faster than my problems can catch me. But more than that, travelling, as in the act of moving from one place to another, is just right. Like my mind is a constant state of tetchiness, an angry alertness that doesn't relax until I'm moving. I feel better in the in-between spaces, I guess.

I wake up. The sun outside is bright enough to creep through the glass tint and curtains. Memories of where I am, and where I am going, pleasantly slide into focus until it gets to the stomach lurching 'why' and I quickly change my mind. I've been on the coach for seven or so hours, though the journey is supposed to be 10 or so hours, maybe? I can't check because the coach doesn't have any Wi-Fi and roaming data is expensive. This is a double pain because it stops my usual morning ritual of looking at social media and various internet feeds, a practice me and an ex (not that one, don't think about that one) used to call 'checking the poles' after the lead character in the book The Wasp Factory's habit of going around the island and examining their fetish shrines for portents and clues. Anyway, I'm happy letting the morning sun hit my face as the road outside the window flies past.

My phone buzzes and the text icon pops up. I thumb it open.

THIS IS A FRAUD ALERT FROM HSBC. WE NEED TO VERIFY RECENT TRANSACTIONS. SHORTLY YOU WILL RECEIVE A MESSAGE WITH DIRECTIONS ON HOW TO RESPOND. WE MAY DECLINE YOUR CARD UNTIL WE HAVE A RESPONSE.

The bottom of my stomach frosts and that cold spreads through my veins. I read it again in disbelief. And again. My card, where's my card? I realise I'm not wearing my body wallet. My bag. I unwind my bag from my legs, where it sits while I sleep in public, and spill the contents onto the seat next to me. The body wallet isn't in there. The cold has reached my brain and my eyes open as wide as they can go, as if sucking in more information will help. The body wallet. Is. not. In. There.

Okay, breathe. You could have packed it in your rucksack. Yeah genius, just like you've never done before? In the top pocket for convenience? You didn't, you know you didn't.

Another message

HSBC FRAUD ALERT: POSSIBLE UNAUTHO-RIZED TRANSACTIONS ON CARD ENDING 123 ₱29955 11:25 AM IF YOU MADE ALL TRANSAC-TIONS REPLY Y, OTHERWISE REPLY N.

Did I try to take nearly 30,00 pesos out of my account on a moving bus, while I was asleep an hour ago?

N

HSBC FRAUD ALERT: WE SUSPECT FRAUD ON YOUR CARD; AN HSBC AGENT WILL CALL YOU SHORTLY.

I root around my bag debris. The body wallet isn't there, was it taken on the bus? No, not if the card was used an hour ago. I quickly push having to accuse the strangers around me, in a language I don't speak, out of my head.

My phone rings and a nice, calm woman, who I suspect was chosen for this exact reason, takes me through some security questions and confirms what the texts told me, but in nice soothing tones rather than panic-inducing block capitals. She cancels my card and tells me the next one will be sent out in the next few days. My stomach does one last icy backflip when I realise I haven't changed my address on the bank account and I will have to contact Her to arrange for my new card to be sent to my mom's house.

Then another thought stomps into my head

My passport.

My passport was in the body wallet. My mind is suddenly a traffic jam of thoughts. Call Mom? How do I get home? What if the bus is stopped? An image of a human trafficker slicing a nun's throat, while running out of an orphanage with his underwear around his ankles springs into my mind. As he penguins away something drops out of his pocket, the Mexican cops pick it up. Tight zoom on my face in the back of a dirty British passport. No Wi-Fi means I'm helpless. No information or way of communicating.

I check my wallet, I have some cash and a travel debit card I can load with money straight from my bank account. I remember the travel agent selling it to me and thinking "I mean, I'll never need it, but sure".

The bus is air-conditioned, the panic sweat is cooling on my skin and making me uncomfortably cold. Logical Method Danny Brain takes over, mentally inventory what I've lost: my passport, my bank card, a chunk of Mexican cash and my emergency two-hundred American dollars. Okay, I figure. The cash is gone, the bank card I can do without as long as I'm smart with transferring money onto the travel back card. The passport is...

Another flip of fear in my stomach.

Well, I don't know, but if my calculations are correct I should be in San Cristobal in an hour. I'll make a list of things I need to find out and do, and deal with it then.

It's been two hours and we haven't stopped. I take an executive decision to pay for the data roaming charges. I check the map and not only are we at least three hours away from San Cristobal, but we're also travelling in the opposite direction. Did I sleep through a stop? When is the next one?

'Don't think about that now.' Logical Method Danny Brain kicks in again. You wanted to get off so you could use the internet. Well you have it now. Focus on the things you can change. After half an hour of reading the only way of cancelling a lost passport is a form I need to print out and post to the home office or consulate, after that I can apply for a new one by post or get an emergency passport. Logical Method Danny Brain signs off for a while. 'I'm tired now' it says, 'If you have to mail the form there isn't an hour/minute deadline to cancel it if you can only do it by post.

My mind slips into the song 'Just' by Radiohead. You do it to yourself, you do, that's what really hurts.

I check the map again, the highway we're on is comically straight. The most efficient way of taking me in completely the wrong fucking direction. Impatience crawls at my skin. This will not do. Buses are my safe time, a timeout from the overwhelming foreignness of travel. I look out of the window. It's disappointingly free from instructions of what I should do, no billboards with step-by-step guides to replacing your passport, no maps of coach routes. I mean, at this point I would have taken a supportive looking stray dog.

The coach is slowing and, if I press my face up against the glass, I can see another checkpoint ahead. What if they check ID - I have literally nothing. The coach pulls up in the queue. Should I pretend to be asleep? They don't always check ID, in fact they are more likely not to, but what if they do? I use some of the precious data to translate "my passport has been stolen" and write it on a piece of paper. Then add the translation for "don't shoot" just in case.

We're waved through.

The bus doesn't turn off the highway. The bus continues to go straight and pointedly in the opposite bloody direction to the one I'm mentally pleading it to go. Eventually, the barriers become less frequent and the surrounding land comes to meet it. The highway becomes a main road and we're in a little hamlet that isn't even marked on the map. The driver stops and pulls off the road into an alley between two low, flat concrete buildings that may or may not be abandoned. Incredibly, some people get off. 'One ticket to Murder alley, Nowhereville please'. This isn't a sanctioned drop off point, and definitely not a bus station. The gap between the coach's door and the wall is about a foot and a half. I watch as a middle-aged Mexican man squeezes sideways down the gap. The driver sits there f for a bit and starts to eat his lunch.

I want to act, do something, but what? I decide that, in this case, nothing is the best thing to do. It's better, I'm still doing nothing but this time it's a strategy. Studying the map, scrolling way ahead, it looks like there is a junction coming up in a couple of hours. If the bus doesn't turn at that junction and head towards San Cristobal, I will get off at the next stop and figure out what to do.

****

The bus turns, and when I get out at San Cristobal the air smells fresh. It has obviously just rained and taken everybody by surprise. Everyone outside the bus station has dripping hair and wet shoulders. Not that I saw it rain, the bus for the last hour has been following steep winding paths down through thick forest, eventually reaching San Christobal de las Casas, named after its patron saint St Christopher and the 16th century bishop Bartolomé de las Casas who wrote about the treatment of the local people and was considered a hero. In the native language it is simply known as Jovel, a tiny town indented into the countryside like a button sewn into a deep fur coat.

In a waiting taxi, I hand the driver a piece of paper with the address of the hostel I've booked. I know you shouldn't just get into random taxis you have not booked but at that point I just don't care, pretty much everything of value has already been nicked. After the taxi fare all I have is my life, my dignity, my honour and a few pesos, and you could trade all that for a packet of chewing gum at best.

He takes the paper and seems equal parts confused and concerned. "Policía?", he asks. I mirror his confusion and take the paper from him. It reads "Il mio passaporto è stato rubato NON TIRARE" (my passport has been stolen DON'T SHOOT). I scramble for the correct piece of paper, he tentatively takes it from me and is visibly relieved when it only has on it an address rather than cryptic pleading.

The roads in San Cristobal are cobbled and for some reason have incredibly high pavements. The taxi is going an oblique way through the fairly sensible grid system and I can't tell if it's to run up the fare or because of the one way system. At this point I don't care, I just want to be at the hostel, talk to the receptionist about the best way to sort this passport thing out, get some food, and de-stress. The taxi pulls up to a huge set of wooden doors painted a burnt orange. Inset is a smaller door, I push on it and it opens easily.

Inside, the front desk is sheltered but part of an open courtyard. An older man is watching a small television under his desk while the large flat screen TV behind him cycles through tourist board promos for San Cristobal and the surrounding area. It's disguised as a magazine-style, current affairs show and the restaurants, shops and clubs it features are very high end, way out of budget for backpackers.

I approach the desk and the desk guy doesn't look up or even acknowledge I'm there. His work top has been hastily pulled over whatever clothes he was wearing that day and has not been adjusted since. He has the air of a bank robber who has knocked out the guard and has now put on his cap to fool passers-by.

Now, as an Englishman I have three tactics to attract the attention of this man without breaking the biggest unwritten rule of Englishness 'don't cause a scene'. I deploy Level One: The Inquisitive Eyebrow Raise While Shuffling Slightly In Case The Staff Members Sight Is Based On Movement. Nope, no reaction. He leaves me no choice, I give him both barrels of Level Two: Leaning Forward With A Polite But Expectant Cough. I give it a couple of ticks for this devastating manoeuvre to really seep in. Still nothing! The utter temerity of the man.

Digging deep, I muster Level Three, believe me I didn't want to but he leaves me no choice: The Jovial But Stern 'Excuse Me'. That got him. Coming away from his tiny black and white telly I tell him I have a booking and show him the number, he checks the system and asks for my passport.

Ah.

I explain it's been stolen and I have literally no other ID. His lack of reaction at all - let alone sympathy - is jarring, but he checks me in anyway. Indifference worked in my favour, but I'm from a country where you'd have to briefly pretend to care. He shows me a large dorm room with thick wooden bunks and large comfy-looking beds with duvets. I put my bags in a locker and briefly gather myself,. Okay, first priority, print the form to cancel my passport. So, I need the Wi-Fi code and ask the desk to print it from an email I send them. Again, to the front desk.

"Excuse me," straight to Level Three, "Do I need a key for the room or a wristband to get in?"

"It's never locked," he shrugs, and turns back to the TV.

"Oh sorry," I continue, "what is the Wi-Fi password?" He doesn't even look round.

"Wi-Fi's broken."

"One last thing, I need to print off a form so I can cancel my passport, would it be possible to print something here?"

"No printing," he says, still not looking around.

"Okay thanks," I say, "you've been a great help."

At that point I realise how free I am. I'm not married to this hostel, I could go elsewhere. But I also reason, those beds, after a few days of sleeping on a sunbed with a sheet, look like deep fried heaven. There's also no guarantee another place will take me without a passport. Two dogs pad over from the back of the hostel. The one dog goes to his blanket, the other, larger dog comes to my feet and rolls on his back head cocked round expectantly, inviting many belly rubs and, honestly, that swings it. And it's not like I've never had troubles with officials before.

****

I'm trying to impress with a fake, travel-weary rock star attitude at the airport check-in procedure. I step to the counter and am greeted by the faux-cheery check-in clerk. After one look into her eyes I give up my weary act, knowing that to really pull it off my soul would have to be as dead as hers. Steeling myself for the inevitable joke - or worse, suppressed giggle - that my passport picture inevitably brings, I try to be charming, cross my fingers and pray to the fickle Airport God for the most holy of holies, an upgrade.

"There's been a problem." Her smile doesn't even fucking flinch. "Your seat's been cancelled". I think at this point I sigh and achieve exactly what I was trying to fake a minute ago. She then promptly disappears to talk to a supervisor and/or have a cup of tea.

At this point everyone else has checked in, even my friend Phil who, while not particularly looking like a terrorist or a smuggler, definitely looks guilty of something. My course tutor is looking at me like I have a holdall full of grenades and a kilo of Moroccan smack up my arse. I tell him to carry on and get in the queue for security, playing the role of grown up with everything under control.

When the check-in clerk gets back she explains that my seat was cancelled because an overzealous co-worker saw there were two Danny Smiths on the flight and cancelled the second one thinking there couldn't possibly be more than one person with the same name in the world. She then goes on to say that her supervisor is going to see if they can fit me on the flight and then sits there trying to engage me in small talk as if they're doing me a favour.

Anyone who's been on a long haul flight will be acquainted with the dry skin, bum sores and the unshakable feeling of discomfort that you get when you're finally allowed off the plane. This, accompanied with the lack of sleep, eight cans of Stella, and the disorientation of flying over several time zones makes the immigration process seem daunting when actually it's not – it's just a long queue with a stern man at the end. In fact, me and Phil are just musing that Purgatory must be a lot like the American immigration hall: not too hot, not too cold, you're not hungry or thirsty, there's art on the walls but it's not that interesting to look at. You're just blandly waiting for your time to leave.

When it does come to my turn, the border guard scans my fingers, nukes my eyes, swipes my passport. Checks, checks again. Puts his hand on the gun strapped to his waist and then tells me to

"Come this way." Shit. On my way to the dreaded 'back room' I manage to catch my course tutor's eye. He is now looking at me like it's a holdall full of Uranium and four kilos of angel dust I have up my arse. God alone knows why I bothered catching his eye, like American immigration would give a monkeys dick about what a course tutor from a limey art university has to say.

The back room is an impossibly high cops' front desk with three rows of incredibly uncomfortable plastic chairs. I note that they're screwed into the ground, possibly to stop you flipping out and attacking them in frustration, but I made it a life rule to never assault an armed cop with crappy furniture, and it's worked up until now. I'm instructed to sit down. After seven hours of sitting down I don't really fancy that, but I do it anyway and spend the next half hour being ignored while I'm trying to work out the name of the Kafka story that my life seems to have become and, more importantly, remember how it ends. All this while trying not to imagine what having two latexed fingers slowly worked up my back passage by a bored-looking nurse would feel like.

After this time I remember that, while not being the nicest guy in the world, I haven't actually done anything wrong and I manage to forget I'm English enough to approach the desk and enquire what's going on.

It turns out that someone with exactly the same name AND birth date is actually a wanted criminal in America and, after politely pointing out that handing your passport with this information on to an armed police officer is not the action of a desperate criminal on the run, the policeman agrees and adds "Our guy is black anyway." They let me go. Without apologising.

I slip on my shades and walk out to 40 or so people looking at me with a mixture of open contempt, pity and hushed awe. I got to be the world-weary rock star after all.

****

Saturday mornings are sedate in San Cristobal. Most mornings are sedate in San Cristobal, just like most afternoons, which are in peak competition with the lazy evenings, which, in turn, are in a dead heat with the quiet nights for the title 'most sedate part of the day'. The air is fresh in the mountains and it's nice to have to take that extra couple of seconds in the morning to decide if you want to take a jacket. I mean, I never do, but it's nice to have a choice.

I'm drifting through, trying to get a handle on the little city. The street I'm on is very touristy but I try not to give myself too hard a time about it, being a tourist and all. All the bars have seats outside and a person giving out menus at the entrance to these areas. Axel Rose screeches out through the mariachi music drifting from these cantinas. Slash's guitar rings over the native hawkers and even cuts the shrill tone of the crossing signal. I follow the sound of Guns & Roses like a cartoon cat that has just been picked up into the air by the smell of a pie cooling on a window sill. I float past a bored juggler and around a tiny lady with more piles of brightly-coloured textiles and garments than you'd expect any person to be able to carry, let alone a pensioner, it's more impressive than the juggler.

The street is filling up now and I'm still following the sound of G N' R. I look up to get my bearings. Every so often in San Cristobal you can look up above the one-storey buildings and see, against a bright blue sky, the deep verdant mountains that surround the city like older brothers at their sister's first concert.

I'm in a place called The Clover before the final chords of 'Welcome To The Jungle' die. Mexican-Irish bars look like Irish bars everywhere in the world, except in Ireland where they just look like bars. In Mexico they almost exclusively play rock and roll and metal music, and have framed pictures of rock stars on the walls where vintage photos of stern men standing in front of a brewery should be. I don't know why part of the Irish stereotype in Mexico appears to include 'Listens to White Zombie' but I'm grateful because there is only so much traditional Irish music you can take before you just want someone to shout about punching a Dracula.

Most of the time it's exciting, knowing you are exactly where you should be, and also perversely thrilling to be witness to things a dirty freak from South Birmingham shouldn't even dream about. Most of the time. Sometimes the knowledge that everyone you love is thousands of miles away is a gut feeling that drags on your bones.

Not often, but sometimes, it's as lonely as it sounds. But in Birmingham right now there are thousands of lonely people watching Strictly Talent On Ice wondering if it'll ever stop raining, and I'm in a Mexican-Irish rock cantina surrounded by mountains, singing to Elvis Costello watching the bar staff dance.

Picturing home helps. Knowing it's in stasis. In fact that's something I have to prepare for: when I finally do get back, nothing will have changed except me. Travelling is intense, dense with sights and sounds and revelations and realisations. Your memory of the time is full and lurid, your memories of home, while comforting, can seem thin, repetitive. If you think it's lonely to travel, try going home.

That's not to say things don't happen. Usually there's at least two or three unbelievable things that occur, a collective cultural experience that you're not part of. One time it was a tornado touching down in the Midlands, just up the road from me. Another was that on live television a reality show contestant lay on the sofa and pleasured herself with a wine bottle. Perhaps the most unbelievable was returning to find the entire country fascinated and enthralled by a cake competition. To be honest when I get back this time they could tell me they've elected a jellyfish as mayor or that cars are now edible and I'll just have to believe them.

My chair rocks forward and I look around to see who's

kicking it so violently. As I do the music cuts out and the TV monitors die. Outside, everyone is quiet and in the distance alarms are going off. An earthquake. If that'd happened in Birmingham I wouldn't have believed it. The bar staff are looking at each other and then start joking, after a minute the music comes back on and life starts again. I burp and there's vomit in the back of my mouth. Could it be eating only the greasy popcorn they serve with your beer for nearly two days could have negative health consequences? Probably not, I decide, it's a side effect from the tremor I expect. Humans are not meant to be oscillated.

****

It's morning and because of the lack of Wi-Fi at the hostel I've taken to getting up and going to a local café. The cafe is called Revolución and is painted heavily red, with vaguely protesting slogans and posters. The Zapatistas, or Ejército Zapatista de Liberación Nacional (EZLN), were a barefoot peasant army that protested and attacked the neolibral overreach of the Mexican government in the mid-nineties. They burned police outposts, freed prisoners and reclaimed ranches for the people. They were beaten back by the Mexican military and chased to the mountains. They still occupy a large portion of the state of Chapas. If they are to be believed they number in the hundreds of thousands and the villages train their own doctors and teachers. With their simple slogan 'good government' and black-masked poetry quoting, pipe smoking leader Subcomandante Marcos, they've become quite an inspiration to us left-leaning anti-authoritarian types the world over. Cafes like this could quite possibly be funding the movement. There are many cafes and restaurants that do, but to support them either financially or with posters or slogans on the walls is still technically illegal, so cafes like this walk a fine line.

The staff put John Lennon on the stereo whenever I'm there and have a habit of cheerily shouting "Chai" (the tea I drink) whenever I go in, or even walk past if they're outside having a cigarette. Today is a quiet day and as I'm enjoying my tea a young boy comes in with a dirty box and brush. I think he's asking to shine my shoes but I'm wearing flip flops. One of the staff runs over, takes a couple of coins from his apron and guides the boy away affectionately by the back of the neck.

****

I'm assured there are 240 steps up to the Virgin Of Guadalupe church on the outskirts of San Christobel but I honestly lost count around step 84 or so. Just getting to the steps is a walk I am ill prepared for. I walked from the centre of the bowl the city is set in, gently curving upwards, past the tourist restaurants and gift shops, past the coffee shops with reclaimed vintage furniture, past even the actual coffee shops for locals and graffitied side streets, to something approaching suburban family homes behind high walls.

I've stopped at what I'm guessing was step 100, lost in my own heavy breath. I know the view will be amazing, the day is warm and the sky blue with white fluffy clouds like the skies in a Dali painting. My brain is itching at me to turn around to take it in but I resist, waiting for the top. Sometimes I do things like that just to see if I can and unusually, this time, I can.

My eyes fixed ahead of me as I methodically dig into the rest of the steps, I see the last one and the church grows from the floor up into my vision. Mustard yellow footings blossom into two white walled towers and a doorway flanked by the same yellow coloured columns, a balcony with a tiny door above the main one, finished with an arch and a gleaming white cross. It's humble, but important. A simple temple in the sky.

I step into the tiled courtyard. Beyond the blue fence that circles it are palm trees and foliage. To my left is a large, green, wooden cross painted with symbols. Including one hand, one foot, and head of Jesus, a golden cup, a rooster, and a step ladder. To my European heathen eyes, it reminds me of tattoos on old punks.

I notice how quiet it is. I rarely wear earphones day-to-day in other countries, happy to hear the rhythm and chatter of the new places, but it's easy for that to become background too. It's only now in the mountains in front of the brilliant white chapel I notice how quiet it is up here, separate, above the bustle.

The silence is amplified in the church itself. The white and mustard continues inside, but in the clinging gloom the mustard colour on the mouldings is transubstan-tiated into gold. The only light in the room not from the double doors is from the framed image of the Virgin Of Guadalupe that is trimmed with green and red neon, these vivid lines slash the marble floor in reflection.

The Virgin Of Guadalupe is a vision of Mary Mother of God that appeared in 1531 to a Native Mexican, a Nahua man Juan Diego. She appeared to him three times and, in his own language, told him to build a temple, healed his uncle, and miraculously painted herself onto his tilma (a traditional piece of native clothing). She is dark skinned and the pattern on her dress is indicative of an Aztec princess, while her mantle of blue is reserved for gods in that culture. The apparition of the Virgin of Guadalupe is a crossover point from the older gods to the Catholicism enforced by the Spanish settlers. For many, it bought native Mexico into the narrative of Catholicism rather than being something forced together. For others, it showed Mary to be the latest incarnation of Tonantzin, our sacred mother of the Aztec religion who left the sky and promised to come back when the act of sacrifice had finished.

There's a number of other figures around the altar: Jesus, a few other guys I don't recognise, and a number of angels that look as if they are attending the shrine rather than part of it, symmetrically placed, kneeling, holding garlands of flowers or just praising in general. Their faces are androgynous and beatific. I'm concentrating on one, following the line of their enraptured face, when a noise cracks the silence. Wings flapping, a startled bird in the rafters, gone by the time I look round.

Looking out through the doors the city is framed, my first look at the view since I started climbing the stairs. The sky is as blue as I expected, but with more cloud. Giant mountain ranges of white dominate, mirrored by the very real and deep green mountains almost silhouetted against them. The city is spilled out under-neath, bigger than I expected, an endless complex of boxes and detail threaded with trees and wires.

It's hard at moments of such breath-taking beauty not to think of life as a string of banality on which pearls of experience and glittering gems of joy are threaded. I have to shake that ugly out of my head. The trick is to find all of it as wondrous, to appreciate the magnificence of a well-placed cup of tea, and the soul-kicking beauty in a rain-streaked window on a Thursday; to 'see heaven in a grain of sand' as Blake advised. Or? or you get lost, another junkie chasing smack highs of meaning, shamboiling from one photo opportunity to another, travelling continents on silly quests? Don't think like that. Stop thinking. Just look.

Looking out through the doors the city is framed perfectly. A sublime end to your worship, to see the world spread out before you like a midsummer picnic. Walking out, something gently bumps the door frame, an angel pinata, busted but still hanging, flapping its tissue wings goodbye as I step into the silent mountain air.

Down the steps is easier, just, and walking down I can see a series of alcoves and benches to the left. The first of these is occupied by two teenage lads, legs crossed over each other, one hand on each other's thigh, trying on each other's hats and sunglasses, finding reasons to touch each other as lovers do. Being LGBTQ, while not illegal in Mexico, is still frowned upon, especially in the shadow of the Catholic church, both figuratively and, in this case, literally. I make eye contact and smile. In that smile I try to communicate so much about under-standing, about solidarity, pride and love. But it's just a smile and even that can get lost in translation.

In the next alcove lies a man, face beaten and swollen. Judging from the swelling and colour of the bruises he copped it a couple of days ago. He's still - too still. I think the worst, this is it, this is what I've been looking for after all. Mr Death's handiwork first-hand. But then a fly lands on his cheek and an eye twitches. I try not to be disappointed. I want to help, but what could I do? So I ignore the list of helpful things forming in my head and allow myself enough pity to feel human but just short of actually doing something. Like the good, finely-calibrated sociopath that years of living in the city have trained me to be, I move on.

****

I'm in a minibus winding through narrow mountain roads. The rainforest that surrounds the roads is hidden in thick morning mist, the driver must be navigating via reflex, memory, luck, or a combination of all three. The thought of this is waking me up better than any coffee. The road turns into a bridge and a gap in the mist means I am suddenly confronted with a drop of a few thousand feet flying by my window.

"Jesus," I say to myself. There's a Canadian couple next to me, and without thinking the man leans across me snapping pictures with his phone. He immediately realises what he's just done, his girlfriend looks mortified.

"Sorry," he says, "I've just never seen a drop like that."

"That's quite alright. I was beginning to think Britain is just tiny and I'm impressed by everything that everybody else finds quite normal."

"No, that was some view," he confirms.

Nathan and Alice introduce themselves, they're both from Canada. Alice is a Geologist so is particularly interested in the tour.

"What's your interest?" she asks. Her accent has a Latina edge.

"I'm looking for Death," I say. They blink.

"At the bottom of a canyon?" asks Nathan. I shrug.

"Sure, what do you think he looks like?" It's Nathan's turn to shrug.

"At the bottom of a canyon, a big fucking crocodile." We all laugh. Alice offers me coffee from a thermos and I get the impression I've been adopted as a pet weirdo for this trip.

We arrive at the carpark and are hurried off into a building that seems to consist of shoulder-high steel barriers like at a theme park. At the end are a bank of life preservers. The rest of the bus are already helping themselves. We look at each other and join in. Me and Alice have clearly put them on before so when we are finished we both help Nathan who has managed to put his on inside out. The building opens up to a jetty with a waiting speedboat and, for some reason, a man playing a comically large xylophone. We're herded onto the speedboat, the benches sit four so we find an empty one and do our best to spread out.

The speed boat's captain gives us a safety lecture, maybe in Spanish, Alice looks round at me and Nathan pretends to listen.

"You too?" she asks me.

"Me too?"

"You don't speak Spanish either right?" she gestures to Nathan who comically shrugs.

"No," I say, "Do you?"

"Yes,"

"Then what did he just say?" gesturing to the guy at front.

"He said that you're both idiots," she teases. Me and Nathan both agree. "He also says not to stand up and keep your hands in the boat"

"Thanks," I say. I mean, he definitely said more than that but I keep quiet.

And we're off, the Sumidero Canyon is at the centre of a national park made up mainly of rainforest. As the speedboat banks around every corner you're hit with stunning beauty. By now, the mist has burnt off and sun catches the edges of sheer cliffs, throwing the lush green foliage that spills down into the shadows and light. Alice turns to me and says

"It's easily as old as the Grand Canyon, you know?" I didn't. "Gaps in the Earth's crust cause the split and the river cracks it open," she says with wonder. She's not translating this, this is all Alice.

"Nerd," Nathan teases, obviously and hopelessly in love. She hits his arm with love right back. It stabs at me, but I'm happy for them, as sad as I am for myself. The captain starts to speak. Alice catches her breath and, instead of translating, hits Nathan again and points.

On the far bank, the huge log that had been floating just under the water blinks and glides to the sandy bank. As it emerges it flexes its huge tail and kicks some dirt with its back leg. The crocodile snaps briefly at something, we're too far away and it was too quick to see individual teeth but a very old part of my brain fills the gaps

The whole boat holds its breath with a few hesitant photos being slyly snapped. I don't know why the hesitancy, it's very clear it knows we're here. The chilling thing it it just doesn't care. It's not there long, within a minute or two it slips into the water with a slick efficiency that is totally at odds with how awkward it looks on land.

Upriver the water looks different, busier. As the boat glides into it we can see that it's thick with refuse - a dense archipelago of pop bottles, crisp packets, food cartons of various decomposition, brown mulch, and carrier bags. It stinks of bins and rot and the air is dense with insects. The trash looks solid, like we could get off and walk to the shore. We cruise through slowly as if making a point. I now realise it wasn't indifference we were getting from the crocodile, it was contempt. Bill Hicks described the Human race as a 'virus with shoes' and that's how it feels, a grubby little species. I wonder how we must have looked to the crocodile? A plastic wrapped, multi-armed organism, brightly coloured to warn the other species how toxic we are, stinking of diesel and roaring about as if we own the place. We move past the debris, but the stink stays with us all a while.

Although there are sandy banks occasionally dotted along the canyon, the majority of time its sheer grey rock surrounds you, beyond your field of vision in all directions. This is a sense anyone from a big city is accustomed to, but here you are encouraged to look up and appreciate the scale. In the city no one looks up but tourists, it's the urban jungle equivalent of drinking at the water hole with a suspicious number of green logs floating in it.

The boat circles for a while before settling against one of these impossibly high faces. Three quarters of the way up a waterfall cascades down the moss-covered wall, the result is a broad skirt of green and erosion. Alice translates the captain, this is the Christmas Tree Falls, so called because the moss and outcrops grow from the water break in a broad triangle. It's hard to see this close up, so when the captain circles us back to take it all in from the opposing bank it does indeed look like a Christmas Tree. Although Pythagoras would be marvelling at the formation of a triangle in nature, Alice is talking Nathan through how the mushroom shaped outcrops are actually formed by mineral deposits. I wonder which lens I should be experiencing this through. Wonder? Awe? Is this what cynical detachment feels like? Tragic self-regard? In geology they think of time in terms of eras, the difference a stream can make in thousands of years. Human culture and lives seem insignificant in comparison. That's how I see these wonders, as a speck.

"Are you alright?" Alice asks.

"Yeah, just tired," I answer.

Around the corner is a cave, the white and grey rock inside shimmers with pink and glints with blue sparkles. Deep in the back crevice is an icon surrounded by flowers with a short ladder underneath it. At first glance it seems impossible to get to but, as we get closer, we can see parts of the wall with worn steps and handholds. Still, this close to the river everything is wet, and getting there to replace the flowers is a true act of agility and devotion. The image is Our Virgin Of Guadalupe. Alice tells us the colours come from the magnesium and potassium deposits in the rock. It's odd, incongruous that in such a theatre of awe humans have bought their tiny god. Deep in the sublime we saw a corner for our own stories and scale, and risk our lives to devote ourselves to it.

At the end of the river is a long municipal works, it's the Chicoasen dam, the biggest in the country Nathan tells us, proud to know something Alice doesn't. We're left to float for a while, under the bright sun.

Before long we're joined by another boat selling beer and crisps. The crisps are salted but served in an open bag with a generous amount of hot sauce. We all buy beer from the boy that spiders between the boats, ferrying the money and cold cans from the coolers.

The beer boat chugs away but stops then waves and shouts for us to hold up. It catches up and the boy jumps aboard to hand something to a surprised looking large dad.

"They short-changed him," Alice confirms.

The speedboat earns its name by full-throttling it back to the beginning, it's like skipping across the top of the water like an expertly thrown stone.

Later, the coach pulls up with a start, waking me. It's only mid-afternoon but the sun and the early start meant as soon as the bus pulled away I was drooling asleep. We're in a car park, at the bottom of which are concrete platforms. The whole thing is dug out of thick foliage, a canopy of plump green that obscures the view until you get to the edge and look over the barriers. During my brief snooze the minibus has climbed the thousands of feet up to the top of the canyon. I get to the balcony and see the view from the other way round. It doesn't seem real through the haze. A blur of not processing the scale, the beauty of it all. It's too big to fit into one tiny head. To orientate myself I look down at the cliff underneath me, the rocks and sparse weeds just underneath my feet, then follow it down, and down, and down. My head swims. In cinema there's an effect called the dolly zoom where the camera zooms in while the camera itself is pulled away. That's what my brain is doing. The world is dolly zooming and I realise how far I am leaning over the edge. Standing straight I can now take it all in, but the spell is cast, nothing seems real. The view, as stunning as it is, is just a well painted backdrop; even the verdant plants seem plastic, too shiny, too lush.

To the left there's a toilet block. I head over and see a big M painted on the door and go in. There are no urinals, which is fine, I go into a stall just as a middle-aged confused woman comes out of the one next to it. She says something in Spanish which I don't need Alice to translate. I leave to see Nathan and Alice laughing.

"M stands for Madre, you want H for Hombre," Alice says through giggles. Shrugging off any embarrassment I go back to the view. The vertigo isn't as bad this time, but there's a thought *That* damned thought, seductive and convincing. Not 'kill yourself' or 'jump,' those could be easily dismissed. No, my self-destruction knows me better. The thought won't leave, as convincing as it is irrational. 'What would it be like to fall?' Time enough to know, not long enough to be scared, just instant acceptance, or not, over in less than a minute. I'm not going to do it - or am I? That step you took could be part of it, part of actually doing it, just another step, what's a step? - but I'm allowing the thought to breathe. My bank card is in my pocket, it's the only ID I own. How would they know who I am? Without my passport, I'm hardly here, a ghost. Would they care? Would the guy at the front desk even stop watching the TV as they root through my belongings looking for a clue? I quickly lock the thought back up and head back up to the van. Besides, if I did do it, they'd all think I did it out of the embarrassment of walking into the Ladies toilets.

****

The next day, another early start and I fight my way through a grey morning drizzle to another minibus and another drive out of San Cristobal. Our guide is an amiable guy, wearing a check flannel shirt, cargo pants, and a less than pristine cap. Atl looks more like a plumber than a tour guide. Only a lanyard gives away his role. He wisely lets the bus wake up before he actually starts guiding the tour. Today, we will be visiting Zinacantan and Chamul, both very traditional townships. Zinacantan is our first village and means 'land of bats' which is probably something to do with the settlers seeing the locals worship a stone icon of a bat. As such the Tzotzil people native to the area have come to be known as 'people of the bat', but in Tzotzil the word 'Tzotzil' means 'wool'. Ironically enough, the Tzotzil language is called 'bats'l'kope' to the Tzotzil, which means 'true word'.

The whole region is the Zapatista heartland and staunchly anti-authoritarian, to the point they refuse to recognise daylight savings time and do not tolerate the presence of state police or military force. Although Atl adds bitterly, "The government will come and take what they want anyway." Apparently, the government has been selling off land and water rights to large corporations.

"Water is a problem in Mexico, not all communities have access, Coca-Cola manufactures here and it takes two and a half litres of water to make one litre of coke. The water, they take from us, and sell it back. And people buy it, we're addicted to the sugar" he throws his hands up with a little exasperated 'ay'.

Soon enough the minibus bounces off the highway and around the dusty roads of a village. Atl points out the school and health centre, saying the law about attending school in Mexico is different but in Zinacantan attendance is much higher and children stay in school longer.

We find the road again and pull up in a town square, it's nice - looks new, with smooth concrete paths and white buildings. Atl climbs out of the driver's seat to address us.

"Just to remind you, the people that live here have lived in this area for over a thousand years, they might stare. You are the strange ones here, this is their home. Ask permission before you photograph anyone, they will probably refuse or ask for money. Whether you give it to them is up to you."

We climb out of the van, the sky is still dark with grey formless clouds covering most of the sky. Sure enough I find a patch of rich blue sky, as blue as your favourite memory of sky. My Nan always said it will always turn out nice if you can find a little bit. "Enough blue to make a pair of sailors trousers'. It's good to be remembering my Nan in what feels like such a remote place, a little bit like she's with me, showing her bits of the world she never got to see. Our minds are powerful. I suppose people don't really die when those that knew them, that cared for them deeply, carry a version of them in their heads. More independent than a memory, more tangible than a ghost, not quite an afterlife for individual consciousness but a way of living nonetheless. The Tibetans have a concept of thought forms, called a 'tulpa'. Complex beings in our minds that we will into existence. When we catch ourselves thinking 'what would Nan have thought about that' or 'I know what Nan would say' I think we're actually updating these tulpas, allowing them to grow with our experience and to continue to develop, making them more real than a static memory or forgotten photograph. It's good to have Nan here, she didn't take any shit.

Atl takes us to a temple, it's a temporary building as the real one is being renovated. It's essentially a large barn-like structure. Atl points out the moss around the doorway.

"When the colonists imposed Catholicism the natives did not abandon the old gods right away, or ever really. They just incorporated the new ones into what they already believed, sometimes they would hide statues of the old gods behind the cross, or just give them new catholic faces. This, over time, got mixed together. For example, the moss is a blessing from the mountains."

The room has rows of traditional looking pews, down each side of the hall runs mismatched tables, on them half a dozen boxes containing statues of different saints. Although each one of these saints is modelled with clothes, each of them is dressed in native tunics and ribbons. The tables in front of the saints are covered in candles. I throw a couple of pesos into a collection box in front of some fresh candles and light one in front of St Lucia and St Christopher. I don't know why, just to say hello really.

"You light a candle when you ask them for something and light one to say thank you," Atl explains. I ask about the clothes and ribbons.

"It's something the women do every so often."

"And what about the mirrors, around their necks?" I ask. Atl has an "aha", and addresses the group.

"Some of you have noticed the mirrors." He points to the mirrors on the neck of a nearby saint.

"Mirrors are one of the old ways I was talking about. A mirror is there to deflect bad spirits and help your soul find its way back after praying." He holds up his lanyard and the back of his ID is mirrored.

The room is thick with incense, distractingly so. The altar is a jumble sale of saints, larger statues, candles, fairy lights and even a figure of Rudolph the Rednosed Reindeer. When the group has gathered near the entrance Atl asks us,

"Did you notice the animals?"

Not one of us did. He gestures to the saints and hidden amongst them are small wooden animals; deer, dogs, lizards, birds, all no bigger than a child's toy. All of them hidden or tucked away.

"The belief is humans have two souls, one of them, the wayhel, is an animal. Each animal is different, a companion. Whatever happens to you happens to your wayhel and the other way round. People put figures of their wayhel with the saints so they are blessed too."

I briefly wonder what my wayhel would be and then remember the huge magpie tattoo on my chest.

Word must have got around because as we get outside a couple of street vendors have pitched up carrying folding wooden displays of jewellery. There are a couple of kids, no more than six or seven, in traditional outfits accepting coins in exchange for photographs. Atl is visibly uncomfortable as the rest of the group browse. I have enough jewellery and, having worked with young people for the last 10 years, I keep a general rule of not having photographs of other people's kids on my phone, so I hang out with Atl. a big blustery woman, a fellow bus passenger from San Francisco, approaches us.

"What is the meaning of amber? Is it protection?"

"It's jewellery" says Atl "We have a lot of it because the mines are close by."

"Is it real," she presses and gestures to the vendors. Atl is clearly torn, on the one hand he knows it probably isn't, on the other he doesn't want to upset the locals and deprive them of their income.

"The mines are close so there's a lot of it around here, but you decide if you buy it or not," he says as he moves towards the van. The way he said it, I wouldn't have chanced it, but the San Fransican woman doesn't get the hint.

Atl leads us over the road and tells us that we are about to see a textile co-operative. "They'll show you around, show you how they make the textiles and how they live."

We're taken through the corridor into a veranda, it's a space between buildings but covered and furnished, and every available space is taken up with a rainbow of material; jumpers, dresses, shirts, blankets, reams of pattern cloth. The group goes into shopping mode immediately. The people in the shop greet Atl like a friend and hand him a cup of coffee in a Winnie the Pooh ceramic mug. He tells the group "These guys will look after you, if you need me I'll be in the kitchen."

A tray of shots appears and we are handed a plastic thimble of local liquor. We 'cheers' and knock it back. Like all local liquors the world over, it's a shade too sweet and tastes vaguely of medicine.

One of the staff here is a younger girl, she's about 14 or so and it's clear she's the only English speaker amongst them. By the weariness of her replies and the deft handling of the group, it is far from her first day. A young American couple from our group are selected to model traditional wedding outfits and they gamely climb into the dress and tunic while the rest of the group takes pictures.

We are shown how the textiles are made by hand and with machine embroidery, it's wildly time-consuming and intricate. We're then ushered into a kitchen. In one of the connecting shacks is a traditional kitchen, the room is matt black, every available surface black. There's a woman by a black pot on the larger black stove, washing and prepping chicken feet before throwing them in the pot. There's another woman methodically pressing wafer thin tortillas in a press on the table. We're given coffee in thick stoneware cups. It's strong, almost syrup, with an ungodly amount of sugar. I visibly wince after sipping and catch the eye of Chicken Foot Woman who breaks a smile and says something.

"Mexicans have a sweet tooth," the girl translates.

We drive a little further to another town. Every so often a loud bang jumps the van, and in places the road is busy with people. Atl tells us we're in Chamula and it's likely to be "rowdy".

"Today is a feast day for St Francis, some people will be drunk and throwing fireworks. It's an old tradition, people used to bang rocks together to scare the bad spirits away, now they use fireworks. I don't know if people know that's why, but people still do it."

Chamula is a lot less polished, rougher. The streets are cobbled, the buildings worn, and as we walk from where we're parked we are pointedly stared at. A procession of men walks past, each dressed in thick, black wool overcoats, buried under these longhaired tunics and flat brimmed hats.

"They're the elders." Atl answers the question before we have to ask. Occasionally, one of the elders looks over daring comments or disapproval, none come.

We get to a large, mostly empty, flagstone courtyard which is dominated by a large white church with forest green trim and mint green accents. Five lines of bright-ly-coloured bunting run from the bell tower overhead to a point across the other side of the square, where a busy market is dealing with the people who have finished watching the procession, drunk men who, to my eyes, are dressed like cowboys but are more likely just wearing clothes, and women and children in traditional dress milling about buying vegetables.

Atl gathers us before we go into the church to explain what we're about to see.

"The first thing to remember is that the people that worship here consider themselves Catholic. The thing they are doing inside, to them, is more like medicine than a part of that Catholicism." He seems defensive but not apologetic. "Most villages wouldn't have regular access to Western medicine but they would have their own healers, someone who knew which plants could make you better, a bone guy, the equivalent of midwife, all these skills are passed on. One of these healers is chosen through dreams or signs - the j'ilol, the one who sees - they can tell by your pulse if you've been affected by a curse or jealous thoughts or what part of your soul is damaged. They know the prayers, candles, or sacrifices to make you better." Atl waits for a reaction for the last one, the group does not react. "This is a place of worship that still has Catholic services, so please be respectful. They will not tolerate photographs."

With that warning I enter the church. It's large and looks more so because of the lack of pews which are heavily absent. It's dark. Halfway up the stone walls, window slits glow white but don't offer any illumination. Instead, the hall glows yellow from the hundreds of candles put before the countless saints entombed in the glass-fronted boxes that line the walls, their carved faces brought to life by the flickering.

The floor is covered in pine boughs which can barely be smelt above the opal incense and candle smoke. The pine is swept away in places to allow for circles of people lighting different coloured candles and praying. Around one of these circles an old woman squats in a pile of black drapery and is talking to a family who occasionally genuflect and mutter prayers. While she talks she sips from a dirty bottle and pours some in a little dish which she places into the net next to her, inside of which is a very tipsy looking chicken.

Atl is standing at the back, he has a rosary in his hands but isn't praying.

"Is that woman giving the chicken booze?" Atl nods.

"It's moonshine called Pocs, she drinks it as part of the medicine."

"But why the chicken, is that part of it?"

"Keeps it calm I expect."

As we talk I see the woman wash the coloured candles in Coca-Cola over a metal bowl, one by one. As she finishes she passes them to the family who light them. She takes another swig of pocs and reaches inside for the chicken who is near asleep in her hands. She passes it in front of the family, who are now praying, and gives it some extra waves in front of the elder gentleman before popping the chicken into her lap and smoothly wringing its neck.

I look for a reaction, the 20 or people using the church didn't see, or care, or both, and the rest of our tour group didn't notice. Atl is looking at me for my reaction. While I'm thinking of exactly what my reaction should be, the old woman is guzzling down Coca-Cola.

"The chicken took the disease or demons from the ill person, then the chicken is killed" says Atl.

"Why the coke?"

"If any bad spirits escaped inside of her she will belch them out." The family are still praying. From behind me another old woman enters the church, she could be the first old woman's sister with the same chestnut lined face and missing teeth. Behind her she's dragging a net full of docile chickens. As it drags across the floor you can see the scuffed marble and remains of colored candle wax. I absent-mindedly take out my notebook and begin to write down what I just saw.

"NO!" shouts someone, an elder wearing one of those shaggy black tunics behind me by the door says something harsh pointing directly at me.

"No writing in here," Atl says urgently.

"I was, err, just leaving anyway - meet you outside?"

"Yes," Atl hisses.

Outside is weird. I've become so accustomed to the smell that the lack of it is jarring and, even overcast, the brightness outside is making the inside of the church seem like a hazy dream.

They consider themselves Catholic? But then I think about Catholicism. This is my body - This is my blood. Isn't that as ridiculous? Christianity is a death cult. Obsessed with your death and afterlife with a Roman execution device as its symbol. Cannibalism and vampirism. A priest holds a chicken. This is my body. A priest taking a swig of moonshine. This is my blood. On the whole I prefer the native medicine, but need neither. I know which parts of my soul are damaged.

I go to take more notes hoping that writing near the church isn't as big a faux pas as writing in it. My pen has finally run out, which is just a coincidence I reassure myself. Walking through the market a woman selling bracelets attracts my attention with a wave, she gestures to the jewellery and I shake my head

"No thanks."

She waves again quickly and sorts through the brightly coloured friendship bracelets and pulls out a black and white one. Which to be fair is as a spooky an assessment of my aesthetic as the coincidence of the pen running out. I buy it and tip heavily.

One of the things I love about surfing wasn't the bits on the board. It's the in-between bits, waiting and watching the ocean trying to decipher the pattern of the waves. Lying on the board watching the world breathe. My legs won't keep me afloat much longer. The world is still breathing. It doesn't care.

6. I Death That's Why They Call It the Blues

"I'd like to check out," I say to the guy behind the desk. He doesn't look up.

"Okay," he says. We both wait until I realise there is literally nothing more involved in that process. I give the hostel dogs one last fuss and step out into the San Cristobal afternoon. The weight of the bag is fine but the weight of being a non-person seems a lot to bear. I have no ID, no visa, no residence. No partner. Shut up.

I barely exist, it's not as freeing as I imagined it to be. At best a bureaucratic hassle, at worst, existentially stressful. I've decided to head to the UK Consulate in Mexico City to get an emergency passport and visa. I can then double back, explore, and be back in Mexico City for Día de los Muertos. To get to Mexico City I have to change in Oaxaca city, so I buy a ticket and book a hostel there for a couple of days.

On the coach I settle in, but I can't be too settled. So far, the coaches in Mexico have been a dice roll of officials, border stops, inspections, and ticket checks. I figure this one will definitely have at least one border stop because it crosses a state line. How the authorities will react to a paperless ghost nonperson is anyone's guess. On the coach I put away a bit of paper money so, if things get really bad, I can offer to 'pay the fine' with a wink and possibly make things worse.

The air conditioning is cold. I put on my scruffy hoodie, screw in my earphones and try to melt into the fabric of my seat as the rainforest silently slides past my window.

We've been travelling all night and we pull into a coach station near what looks like an industrial estate. The lights flicker on and the coach's occupants blink awake. Every so often at a coach stop a state police official will get on and methodically walk the aisle filming each face. The officer gets on, a young chap giving off 'I don't like this any more than you' vibes. He dutifully pans the camera left and right at every set of seats. As he gets to me, he gestures to me then points to himself. Here we go. I pop out my earphones. I have no documents and speak no Spanish. I'm in for an incredibly complicated and embarrassing night. He gestures again. Not the earbuds, he's moving his hand over his head. My hair, my pink hair. He smiles. He likes my hair. I suppose his excitement is understandable if you take into account that a large portion of his job is walking up and down coach aisles looking at the top of people's heads. I smile back and he disappears. The coach still isn't moving though. He's got back on and he's got another officer with him. We lock eyes, he's heading straight for me. Balls. He gets to me and gestures to his friend who holds up a camera. He wants a picture with me? He leans in and we smile.

"Gracias," he says, I hold up a finger. Wait. I pull my hair out of my jumper and ruffle it out giving him the full Muppet. He loves it. Another photo is taken and they're off. The coach pulls away, making it very clear to me, and everyone else on the bus my photo op was, in fact, the hold up.

A little after dawn we're stopped again on the highway. An officer gets on, a different uniform this time. Uniformed people are gathered around the entrance - all of them have guns. The officer says something, everybody on the coach is holding up papers and driving licenses for inspection. I hold up my coach ticket and a map of the bars of San Cristobal carefully monitoring my eye contact to 'bored tourist' rather than 'panicking drifter'. He doesn't pause as he walks past me.

It's late when I get into Oaxaca. Luckily, I've booked my room online and copied the address down on paper so I jump straight into a taxi. The taxi finds its way to a square busy with little bars, the music of them mixing with the mill and hum of people laughing and chatting. Mexicans are funny, their voices pitch and roll, they deliver jokes with silly voices and dramatic pauses. They laugh easily, loudly and leave no one out. It's nice here.

The doors and mouldings of the hostel are painted a stylish matt black. I ring the doorbell and state my name, the door buzzes and I push myself into a courtyard room. The walls are covered in a million messages of thanks, tags, and smiles. A massive dog bounds out, happy to see me in the wonderful way dogs manage to be happy to see everyone. Shortly after, in jogs a man wearing clothes both thick knitted and stylish that only the Nordic and this guy can pull off. He shakes my hand, introduces himself as Pieter and seems genuinely pleased to see me in a way that is quite touching after this long on the road.

"Don't mind him, he loves new people. Let's go through to reception and we can book you in." We enter into an office; it's softly lit and covered in rugs. I notice Petrie is in his socks. Through the glass door I can see a kitchen full of people doing shots and laughing.

"It's newbie night - I'll get you booked in and you can put your bag away and meet everyone if you like?"

"Great," I say. Pieter confirms my name and the dates I've booked.

"And I just need to scan your passport."

"Ahh," I say.

"Ahh?" he asks. I tell him how my passport was stolen, he looks concerned.

"Do you have a driving license?"

"No, no ID. I have a bank card and cash, I can pay in advance even leave a deposit." Behind him the party continues and everyone laughs.

"It's the system," says Pieter, "we have no way of checking you in without a scan of your ID. It's a security thing, most places have it." He swings the monitor around so I can see the gap where the scan should go.

"No way at all?" I can hear how panicked I sound.

"No, sorry" he seems genuinely sorry which makes me want to be here more. He sees me glance at the clock. 10:35. Late.

"I'm going to phone around some places, see if you can get anywhere to take you." But I don't want another place, I want to be laughing in the kitchen, petting the huge dog. I want to be here.

"Thank you," I say and Pieter's off speaking in fluent Spanish on the phone as he steps into the back room. With Peiter gone the dog gets up and sits at my feet. I reach down to pet him, he looks up and solemnly licks my face once. It's okay. You'll be okay. Shortly, Pieter comes out of the back room.

"Okay, I've got you a place, there's someone waiting to book you in. I can refund you your deposit or, if you like, I can pay the taxi to the new place, it's about the same?"

"That's great."

Pieter sees me to the cab, carries my rucksack and puts it in the boot as I slink into the back seat. He leans in and speaks rapid fire Spanish back and forth with the taxi driver. He hands him some money and we set off. Old brick and yellow lights pass the window. I just want to be in bed, any bed. Not true, Her bed. Our bed. The driver asks me something in Spanish, catching my eyes in the rear-view mirror.

"No habla Español lo siento." I say. He asks again, I mime how little I understand and how sorry I am in a cringing shrug. We drive around the block two, three times. He's talking to me the entire time; I don't understand the words, but I know he's asking where he should be dropping me off. I realise I genuinely don't know, Pieter organised all this, I didn't even ask the name of the new hostel. The streets are empty and doors heavily blocked, shuttered and closed. Exasperated, he makes a phone call, then another. I'm sure I can hear Pieter and the party behind him. He writes something down on a scrap of paper, we go around the block again and then down a block to an equally closed street.

The driver pulls up finally and gives me the scrap of paper. The journey is finished. I get out and go to the boot for my rucksack. I'm barely at the rear light when the taxi pulls away.

"Hey," I shout. I run after the taxi down the middle of the street waving, hoping he sees me in the rear-view, praying this is an accident and not an incredibly elaborate rucksack heist involving a knit-wear cladded man, a taxi driver and a large dog. At the end of the block he stops and I run harder, maybe he saw me, maybe it's just the intersection. I get to the car and flip the boot open.

"My bag," I shout through to the driver as I pull it out. The driver is still saying something as I slam the boot closed. He pulls off leaving me in the middle of an empty street, in a city I don't know, with no sign of the hostel. I feel a wave of self-pity and an edge of panic. I should be home. With Her. I'm sitting in the gutter. Okay, I'm not sleeping in the gutter, I've decided It'd be a great story, if a little clichéd. I look at the scrap of paper. It's an address without a name. I have a building number, 144, but can't see any numbers on the buildings. I decide to make some assumptions. First this is the right street and right section of street in the grid-like section of the city. Second, even though there's not a massive sign, there has to be something telling people it's a hostel. Taking my rucksack, I methodically walk down one side of the street, no numbers, then the other side of the street Two doors down is what looks like a hardware store, number 140, I back up and examine the doors two behind then two ahead. Set flush against the wall two doors ahead is a set of double doors with an intercom. There're no windows, no signs, but the intercom is labelled 'hostel'.

I buzz the button and a small door, set into the bigger door, buzzes open. Inside is a courtyard with tables and balconies with doors surrounding it. I slump with relief at the desk, a woman in jogging shorts and a cardigan comes.

"Danny?"

"Yes, Pieter phoned ahead? I'm the guy with no passport."

"Yes, he said. Fill these out," she hands me the paperwork. "I'll show you to your bed".

No Wi-Fi in the rooms, no plugs either. The doors don't lock and no dog. I suspect the occupants are mostly migrant workers. I make my bed and let sleep shuffle in. My suspicions are confirmed when I'm woken a few hours later by the sound of the three other men in my dorm trying very hard not to make too much noise as they get ready for work. I'm now alone. Crushed, smothered. I can't decide my next move. I'm here on a mission, I have all this opportunity, privilege, a world to explore. But I can only make it to the toilet and back. I'm disgusted with myself. Was I really going back to sleep?

Yes.

The sun is out and I'm drifting untethered. Exploring is the wrong word, or at least a by-product of what I'm doing. I'm trying to head towards the centre of the city but avoiding the roads with the most people, like sneaking up on a feral animal by standing downwind and sideling into their blind spot. Before I can avoid it, I'm swallowed by a market.

Markets in Mexico are amorphous symbiotes that live in the city's body. They start in the sections or square allotted, but slowly spread. Tarpaulin and steel structures spilling onto the pavements, along the roads until they meet each other and merge. They eat humans whole, beguiling them by taking away all reference points that aren't market. Sheet plastics blot out the sky. Racks of baubles, displays of the stolen, the fake, the cheap all around. Confused, the human will stumble around eventually sucked of all its useful cash nutrients and spat out.

Normally I don't mind. I like the markets, the noise, the baubles, but today it's too close, too invasive. I walk by a stall selling toys: dolls, guns, cheap fidget spinners. Hanging from the back are skipping ropes. I see a plastic neon green one. I catch my breath; I did not need to see that today. Walking the block out, I'm heading to a road crossing which usually gives a break in the stalls big enough for me to work out where I am. But I smell something that rings a bell between my stomach and crotch. Meat. Lots of meat.

The building I'm next to is a food market. I realise just how hungry I am. Spotting a gap I squeeze past, almost knocking a rack of handbags down. The food market is okay, mostly seafood with the occasional table. Then I notice smoke billowing from around a corner, then the sound, like an army of snakes fighting, every so often a high, urgent hiss joins the background sizzle. As I approach there's that smell again: fire and charcoal, with urgent distracting notes of raw, dead flesh.

As I turn the corner, I see the meat market. A corridor essentially. High roofed, the rafters lost in billowing smoke, on each side are the stalls, basically the same stall repeated. Hanging meat, cuts, sausage sliced and prepared on site, diagonal griddles pssting at you like every cut of meat is trying to tell you a secret. I squeeze into one of the five or six high tables packed between the stalls. A man from the grill comes over and says something that sounds like a question.

"Si" I say, and he writes down a large number '9' on his pad. Ten minutes later he brings over a large platter of meat still fizzing from the grill, there are no knives or forks, just a plate of tortilla to pick the food up with.

Pleasure, true pleasure, has the ability to lose the conscious mind, an indulgence into the sensory. Carnality in its truest root meaning. I'm handed a Mexican coke and take a swig, a frying pan of sugar hitting my face. This whole thing is like a cartoon: vivid, immersive, realer than real. I don't remember much of eating; I do remember waddling away dazed and sweating.

I'm sitting in the courtyard of the hostel with a six-pack of beer I bought on the way home. The good thing about hostels is there's nearly always company. Sit in the communal areas with booze and people will normally join. The sun goes down and the yellow sodium lights go up at the same rate. I don't have a watch but it's four beers later and nobody has walked past. That green skipping rope. Why here? Fuck rhetorical questions, who am I asking? God? Myself? There's a reason I'm after Death and not God. I've got a separate set of questions for God. And they revolve around a neon green plastic skipping rope.

****

I'm on duty. We rotate the duty so we only have to do it twice a week. The rest of the councillors are supposed to be 'prepping' for their classes and electives, but the schedule at camp is so hectic - from getting the kids up in the morning to settling them after a day of running activities - that we rarely prep anything in this extra half an hour. And with this damned heat, I bet if I was to open the staff room right now I'd find them all draped over the furniture, napping the afternoon off.

Duty isn't so bad, it's the kids free time and it's good to mix with the sides of camp you wouldn't normally get to. I'm over by the girls' side of the playground. It's interesting to see the kids play. They're from the poor areas of New Jersey; some play well, a product of having a lot of unsupervised time on their hands, some need help, grown-up too fast and never really had time to just be themselves as kids. Teacher sense is a thing, and if you've been around kids for a time you pick it up real fast. There's something about how the kids around the monkey bars are paused: some are side-eying what's going on, some pointedly not looking. I'm running over before three kids break off and run towards me. When I get there, a girl is crying on the ladder. At one end her foot is off the rung, her one hand is grasping at the bars overhead and at the green plastic skipping rope that is tied to them, the other end knotted around her neck.

I've never covered a distance so quickly. Before I know it, I've bundled her in my arms, one of my hands scrabbling to undo the knot around her throat. She's sobbing big racking sobs, her wet face pressed against my chest. She's around nine but weighs nothing. I can hear her saying something but can't make it out. Miss Sharon arrives, head councillor and one of the strongest women I've ever met. She's taking the girl off me. Now that she's out from my arms I can hear what she's saying. Repeating.

"I don't want to go home, please don't send me home."

****

At quarter past five beers, I go to my bunk and hope in the morning I will wake up somewhere other than this formica purgatory.

Sometimes, when you wake up your brain resets. Yesterday and the stuff that seemed so overwhelming and crushing are just thoughts. Sleep has ordered your feelings, cataloguing them and, ultimately, filing them in the 'things that exist only in your head so it's okay' file.

This is not one of those times. I've claimed the bottom bunk and hung towels and sheets around it, my own cave of melancholy. I pretend to sleep until everybody leaves and I spend the day watching inconsequential American TV on my phone. I've failed Oaxaca. Overwhelmed and ungrateful, a non-person slipping through the gaps.

Soon I have no food, no water, and I realise I haven't consumed anything even resembling such since the cans of Tecate Light I had in the courtyard last night. Wearing my bed shorts and my comfort hoodie I poke out into the warm autumn night. Everything is closed, I think it's Sunday, and quite late on a Sunday at that. The list racks up - evidence of a non-functioning human brought to you by the privilege pity party. The streets are empty. I can hear music and people though. On the straight roads I glimpse people and lights just far enough away. I find myself drawn towards them.

The main square and in it is a busy fiesta. There are stalls, food carts, three stages with two bands playing 300 yards away from each other. Already the crowds are thickening around me. I walk the square, another face in the crowd. The two bands are playing at the same time and the audiences of the two are merging, making it possible to start dancing to one band but end up in the others pit. It's loud but not drowning out the knife thoughts. Alone in a crowd, a cliche. There are families buying balloons and vendors selling bubble machines and rainbows pinned to dirty steel tubing. No skipping ropes. My friends have families now, jobs, futures, a timeline in which they are firmly placed, a trajectory. I never wanted that, never thought I did. Until I did, until I found my own 'forever after'. And then it was gone.

I'm happy for my friends, I really am, but being happy for them only underlines what they have and what I've lost. Taken.

Around the corner from the square, different groups take their spots. Older guys around chess boards set up on the corner of the concrete planters, a line of VW beetles reconditioned and admired, large fighting dogs greeting each other with the same enthusiasm as their owners but with a little less hair gel.

I wander lonely like a clown and find I've done a circuit. I'm back where I started, caught between the two bands. The noise is confusing, distracting. I've been crying I think, I think maybe I still am. One band finishes the song and the stamping and spinning doesn't stop as they continue to dance to the other band. I'm crying but I'm on a trip some people only get to dream of. I'm a failure, even at travelling, which makes me laugh, or cry, more. Both. I don't know at this point. To my left is a cathedral, lit in blue. The light makes it look unreal, a movie set. It feels like a spy film when a diplomat is murdered in the crowd but nobody notices because everyone is so busy. I try to melt into the crowd like the killer spy because the alternative is drop to my knees and wait for a passerby to check on me, and then scream as the overhead shot pans out.

Around the back of the cathedral the dog friends have converged around a burger cart. I'm not hungry, I don't think, but I join the queue as an excuse to pet the dogs. The nearest, a pitbull, black, all muscle and shining black eyes pads over, tail wagging. The tug on his chain alerts his human who looks over at me.

"May I?" I say in English and wave my hand near the

dog. The human breaks into a grin and nods yes. I think the dog understands. At the nod she jumps up my legs and when I sit on my haunches, she lands her front paws on my knees nearly knocking me over and licking the tears from my face. I'm laughing. It's often said we, as humans, don't deserve dogs. My theory of cat people and dog people is similar. The people that really love cats over dogs seem to be the cynical, more considered type. People suspicious of love you don't have to earn. To prefer dogs is to be ready for unconditional love. I'd always been a cat person until a year ago when we got a puppy, a perfect tiny dog called Iggy. We slept in the living room on an inflatable mattress for a week just to be next to her cage when she first arrived. A family complete. Next to Her I've never loved anything as much as Iggy Pup. It made sense for Her to keep Iggy. But losing that future, the three of us, still seems brutal.

The pitbull has taken to licking my face then swinging her body around into me so I can rub her belly with a little bark of appreciation.

With almost no negotiation I'm handed a burger and I give the man at the stall some money. Standing up, the dog owner catches my eye and shakes my free hand.

"She likes you," he says. He's wearing a sports vest over a full chest and heavy gold chain.

"It's mutual" I say back, I gesture to the burger and the dog "may I?"

"Nah man," he says with a smile and bends down to rub her flank in the way she taught me too "she's on a special diet." The dog gives a bark which I take to mean "don't listen to this man" but I take a bite of the burger.

It's hands down the best burger I've tasted.

"He's good right?" says the dog owner, I just nod and take another bite

"Tono," he shouts to the man behind the cart who looks up from his concentration "you got another fan." He says it again in Spanish and the man grins before getting back to work.

"It was nice to meet you," I say and shake his hand again, and I mean it.

"Hey man, I hope you feel better," he says kindly. And I do, better, more grounded, dragged from under an avalanche. I'm a little embarrassed it was so obvious, so I hurry up the road away from the fiesta.

There's a book 'McCarthy's Bar' in which Pete McCarthy posits the travel rule if you see a pub or bar with your name on it - you have to go in. Ever since I've followed that rule, I also go and have a drink in any bar or pub called McCarthy's or any that begins with "Mc", just to be sure. So I find myself in an Irish pub hidden in a mostly closed shopping complex.

And after meeting the dog and her owner a little more company would be nice so I sit at the bar nodding at the couple of obvious Americans already there. Now, I'm not being unfair presuming they're Americans because either they're Americans, or they've come to the fiesta in convincing American costumes: large sport shorts, baggy T-shirts, and backwards baseball caps, which, admittedly, is a bit on the nose. One is dressed in mostly white, the other near shades of red. I'm expecting their friend dressed in blue to come meet them the entire time, although he sadly never comes.

I'm preparing some sports chat, which means watching baseball. It seems it's the bottom of the ninth and Oaxaca just stole third on a bunt and as long as I'm not asked any follow up question I'll be fine. I needn't have bothered. The two Americans are both scrolling through their phones, Blanco nudges Rojo.

"Remember the Ewok?"

"Yeah?"

"I banged her."

"Dude?"

"Banged her too," he keeps swiping. "Didn't bang her - but should have."

I'm served and I quickly move away from the bar. My head is still swimming slightly but loud music and my own corner is helping.

"Excuse us, can we join?"

They look like students, nice ones. The woman has thick curly hair, she introduces herself as Gabriella, "Gabby". Peter has round rimless glasses and a dashing scarf, he does most of the translating. Gabby has the confidence and Peter has the English. Still, even with Peter doing his damnedest, most of the conversation is patched together with Google Translate and mime. The third student is Jesus, who is, well, fucked. The sort of drunk where he drifts in and out of focus - he wakes up to join a toast and to apologise how bad his English is, despite saying very little.

Peter and Gabby are lawyers. I ask if they are celebrating anything in particular and they're not really, they are just joining in with the fiesta. They ask why I'm in Mexico. I type "I'm looking for Death" into my phone and show them the translation. They look confused. You want to die? Gabby looks concerned for me, Peter looks worried for them, and Jesus has been trying to focus on the back of a 'no smoking' sign for 10 minutes. I shake my head and smile and type "Grim Reaper" into the little translation box and show it to them. Jesus comes to and looks at it.

"Las Calaca," he says. Peter and Gabby talk amongst themselves confused, but no longer concerned, while I scan read the wiki entry. 'Calaca' is the wonderfully onomatopoeic word in Spanish for skeleton 'Se lo lleva la calaca' is a euphemism for 'death took him'.

"Si, las Calaca," I say. "What do you think he looks like??

"Las Calaca?" asks Peter, I say yes. He shows me the phone "a cloud with a face" in the translation box. Gabby thinks she shows me "kind, with flowers". Jesus comes round again.

"Gringos," he says. Gabby looks shocked, Peter goes to translate, but I laugh. Relieved, Peter joins in and then Gabby too. We toast. While talking about Mexico, Peter explains how he struggles because of how important it is to be 'macho'. I tell him it's hard to be macho with long pink hair, pointing at my head. We laugh and, as he translates to Gabby, I do bodybuilder poses which sets Peter off again.

\

At this point Gabby is looking after Jesus. I order water from the waitress and we slyly replace his beer with it. Peter watches us and asks me if I think Gabby is beautiful. There is a slight edge to the question. I translate "you are a very lucky man" and this seems the right answer. Gabby flashes me a look of awkward apology. Jesus is getting worse, so they need to go. I can see Peter is struggling to translate something while Gabby is rousing Jesus. Peter stumbles over to a group of ladies nearby, interrupting them asking for an English speaker. He returns with a confused looking girl in a pink tracksuit and straight, black-plaited hair.

"He says he 'hopes you enjoy your time here and that you come again'". Peter is as triumphant as she is confused by having to translate such a relatively simple phrase.

"Gracisas," I say, and lean into the accent and sincerity. I mean it; for a while I wasn't a broken puppet on a mission, I was a guy in a bar.

When I get back to my hostel, it's empty again, but somewhere I can hear someone singing 'My Way' in Spanish, badly, but with gusto.

****

My ticket says 10:15 but the board doesn't have a coach leaving at that time. I show my ticket to one of the attendants who points out it's only half nine. I wait. It's 10 past 10 and no coach has been called so I go back to the gates again. The attendant looks confused, then a second attendant looks and snatches the ticket out his hands. He motions for me to follow and sets off. I shoulder my bag and rucksack, and jog heavily after him. He points to a separate, fancier waiting room with its own departure board. As I get near, more attendants take my rucksack from my back. I'm shown to the front of the coach, the driver hands me a bottle of water and illuminates the steps of the coach with a small torch he has in other hand. It seems I've accidently bought a ticket to a premium coach. The main Mexican ATO coaches are good to begin with, but the premium coach has tiny touches which earns its title. The leather seats recline with a rising footrest without imposing on the seats behind. It has free and very strong Wi-Fi, and a jack for the television screens with a choice of radio stations. But the real bonus it seems is unmolested passage through checkpoints and security stops.

Next stop, Mexico city. I'm currently reading a couple of books I picked up on the way: 'Down & Delirious In Mexico City' by Daniel Hernandez and 'How We Die: Reflections of Life's Final Chapter' by Sherwin B. Nuland. Not only am I getting a detailed breakdown of the bandits, kidnappings, muggings and underbelly of Mexico City, but also a graphic description of what it would feel like to die. In the darkest part of night, in a temperature-controlled shell gliding into the most densely populated city in the world, I question my mission. Do I really want to meet Death? I've been watching from far away as the casket of my old life has been thrown into a lake and slowly filled with rocks. Death, like all change, hurts. Not a thousand sunsets or a dozen beers, or any new chewing gum flavours do anything to dull that. Wherever you go, there you are.

Death, real death, is out there. Me bleeding out in an alley clutching my belly is out there. Do I have to die to get the answers? Is that what I've always thought? Is this whole thing just a veiled and expensive suicide run? Either way, the die are cast. No retreat. Even if I wanted to go home, I have to go to Mexico City to get my passport and visa. The only way out is through. And I can't help but feel, like Orpheus, if I look back now, I could lose everything. The honest truth is I don't want a new future, I like my old future. So, what am I even doing? Am I looking for Las Calaca for an answer? Or to challenge him to a chess match for my old life?

You can still move your arms after you have no feeling in them, you just have to imagine the signals you would normally send to them, and trust they go there. Legs too. How can a thing be numb and still hurt? I hope I pass out soon so this can be over.

7. Raindrops Keep Falling On My Dead

The hostel is closed. I lean with my head against the 'open 24 hours' sign for irony's sake and eyeball the taxi drivers of the electric taxi rank opposite, who, in fairness, are eyeballing me right back. I doze standing up for a while, clinging to the doorway like a buoyancy aid. Eventually, a security guard appears. The good news is I can leave my bag in the luggage room, the bad news is check in isn't until two and I will definitely need my passport.

I'm lighter without my bag. As neither the hostel foyer or cafe isn't open yet I stand in the doorway using the Wi-Fi to complete the form for my emergency passport and book the meeting at the embassy for 10am. The map I just downloaded tells me it's a 50 minute walk away, which, if I set off now, gives me half an hour to find somewhere on the way to get my new passport photos done.

The streets of central Mexico are wet in the morning, scrubbed clean slates. I share them with the occasional police officer or hurried looking shop assistant on their way to open up. This time in the morning smells of hot garbage and swamp. Until it doesn't, then it smells of bleach, sandalwood, or freshly cut flowers or hot cinnamon bread. It's good to see the city waking up; intimate, like watching someone dressing in the morning from the bed you shared. Going from a maze of shutters and puddles to people and glass. You don't get to see the sunrise, but you get to see the faces of the city's skyscrapers turn from red to pink, and eventually light up with the innocence of a cloudless baby blue sky. It's a privilege to watch the shadows warp and retreat like blankets kicked off at the thought of a fresh day.

Commerce drives Mexico City, everywhere is a shop with markets spilling onto the streets. The pleasing grids normal in American cities twisted by roads, new paths and residential squares reclaimed from the urban mess. I'm making good time to the embassy, so I divert to what looks like a high street hoping for a Snappy Snaps or Mexican equivalent. Maybe a pharmacy like Boots? They'd have photo booths, right? Or maybe that doesn't translate. I realise a photobooth in a pharmacy makes no more sense than a cobbler does cutting keys as a side business. In Mexico there are so many shops that the same types of business clang together in that capitalist magnetism that turns competing antique shops into the antique district. Looking around it would seem I'm in the Industrial Food Service Equipment District, or, as Birmingham City Council would rebrand it 'The Kitchen Quarter'. As my friend Jon says, "capitalism disappoints".

I search the map for 'photos' and a shop a couple of streets away pings up. I hurry over and it's closed, but even if it was open it only sold photo frames and albums. I've wasted my fuckaround time and I've got to get there now to be on time. I follow the map, lightly jogging to a leafy suburb with high walls and lots of discrete security cameras. I arrive sweating but making up time. I need water. There's a greengrocer in the nearby square, behind the counter is a four-square photo with a price.

"You do photos?"

"Fotos, si."

"I need photos." The old man takes me to the back of the store, shifts some boxes and points to a cupboard. Inside is a stool and a professional pull down background. I sit down and he returns with an expensive looking camera. Five minutes later I'm presented with four tiny professional pictures of a thin, tanned convict that bears a passing resemblance to me. Capitalism disappoints, but sometimes it delivers.

Rita is cheery and understanding, nice enough to make me forget there are two inches of bullet proof plastic between us and two armed guards outside the sliding door. She processes my forms for an emergency passport and extracts the story of how I lost the original while making sure each stage of the process isn't overwhelming for my dyslexic brain. She smiles a lot and, even though she's dressed professionally I can see her arm is covered in vivid flower tattoos. She disappears for a while and comes back to tell me there's a problem with the printer. I explain I can't check into the hostel, or indeed, any hostel, without a passport. Rita thinks.

"Wait there." When Rita comes back she has a letter from the embassy itself explaining the situation. It has a flowery signature, is stamped and embossed with a fancy seal. "Will this help?". I tell her it will and promise to come back tomorrow.

The walk back seems shorter than the walk to the embassy, a fact that is often documented and probably has a solid psychological explanation and even a fancy, German, compound word name. The effect is made all the more pronounced in this instance by me needing a poo quite badly.

*****

I meet Paul while waiting for the coach in Udaipur. I was sitting on a concrete bench, stewing in a flop sweat and being bullied by some local children. I'm clearly not well and so very not prepared for travel with no clean clothes, a fever, and a stomach that's choosing to eject anything it's introduced to in an upwards/downwards roulette. Paul is a lovely bloke with foppish haircut. A good school type, taking a year to travel before applying for the bar. Anyway, it's Paul who chases the kids off, Paul who gets us a bed for the night when the coach makes an unexpected overnight stop in Aminabad, and Paul who is now shouting up the stairs for me so we can meet our pick up to get back on that coach. I bounce downstairs feeling pretty good. Last night I ran to a nearby market and bought a fresh pair of shorts and spare underwear.

"We're being picked up in a minute," says Paul. I gesture to the manager who has chosen to join us at the door while we wait.

"Why is he here?" I ask.

"No idea." The manager just smiles and spreads his hands like a stage magician. I feel a cramp. No, please. Then another.

"You okay?" Paul asks.

"Sure," I say. But I was not okay. The cramps had given away to a terrible pressure in my guts. It's just wind, I lie to myself. Just let it squeak out.

It isn't wind.

"Actually mate, I think I left something in the room, watch my bag and I'll run up?"

"You want me to go get it?"

"Nah I'll go," I say. Peter looks confused but I'm already waddling confidently up the stairs. I get to the bathroom in our room. The damage is confined to the underwear, so I take them off and clean myself up, regrettably leaving the soiled boxers in the bin. The rest of my new underwear is now packed downstairs in my rucksack so I chance going commando. I do feel much better, like that was the last bit of badness I needed to expel.

"You okay?" asks Paul.

"I am now," I say, leaving no doubt about what just happened.

The coach comes and we stuff our rucksacks into the hold. I find my seat; I've forgotten I splashed out on an upgrade. My seat is a sleeper seat: a bench seat running parallel to the window with no back and a plastic vinyl mattress. Not quite large enough to lie flat, but nowhere near comfortable enough to sit up on. Especially until we get to Goa. I try folding various limbs and different positions, ignoring various stares from the other passengers, when I feel more than hear it RRRRRRRIIIIP!

The shorts, the cheap ass, paper-thin Indian market shorts. I subtly grope around for the damage. The inside seam has ripped open from the hem of one leg cuff to the other. And I'm not wearing any underwear. Unless I trap the material between my legs, my arse, cock and balls are on display, framed by hair and the world's most rubbish shorts.

"Paul?"

"Yeah mate?"

"How long are we on this bus?"

"Oh, about ten hours, why? You okay?" I look down at the disaster beneath my waist.

"Fine."

****

Check-in goes well, even without the passport with the letter I got from Rita I could probably check into the mayor's house. The hostel is an old modernist building with marble walls and the rooms of each floor surround a central atrium. The rooms are nice and clean. Neat. My guts are cramping. In the room I'm in I spot two beds already taken, luckily both roommates are both out. I run to the toilet. The lock sticks but my guts have an urgent deadline, so I turn the latch with a heavy crunch, desperation and frustration adding a little more leverage than I perhaps would normally.

Cramps. Expulsion. Relief.

The toilets in Mexico have a little sign explaining that the Mexican sewage system can't handle toilet paper and, once used, it goes in the little bin kept under the sink. These signs are usually in English, presumably because Mexicans already know this. I'm considering this as I pull myself together, washing my hands and unlocking the door. Except the door won't unlock. In fact, the latch is just spinning around in its casing, not affecting the lockedness of the door one bit. Rather than a list of options of what to do, at this point I have a list of things I really don't want to do. Near the top of that list is phoning down to the front desk and explaining to someone who barely speaks English that they need to break me out of the room after I've made a smell like I've been dissolving stray dogs in stomach bleach. I'd rather stick my hand in the shit paper bin and look for a key that I know doesn't exist.

I look at the lock again, the latch is free spinning, and juggling free from its casing. The casing is flat to the door but not totally flush with tiny screws. One of my rings looks silver but is actually steel, I fit the corner of it into the screw and unscrew the panel from the door. Assorted lock parts fall to the floor. I ignore them and, stabbing around in the lock itself, I can feel the lever that drops the dead latch. I grab a bit of metal from the floor and lever the drop latch open. The most pathetic part of all of this is not the pride I felt, but the thought 'Just like BA Baracus would have done.' As if there was an episode of the A-Team where the gang gets the trots and are locked in a toilet.

At the front desk I drop the assorted broken lock parts onto the desk.

"I was locked in the toilet," I say. The man on the front desk pauses, thinking about it. There isn't a lot you can say too that.

"The door of the toilet in my room is broken," I reiterate. "There it is, most of it"

"Would you like a new one?" the man says.

"A new room or a new lock?" I ask. The man pauses for a beat.

"Either?"

"A new room, please."

My new room has been recently renovated and the whole floor is empty while the rest of its rooms are fixed up. I shower and go to the rooftop bar where the beer is ice cold and the view of the rooftops around me seems hyper-real: a million details in sharp focus, vents and pipes, the fritzing back of a neon sign, struts, nuts and spouts. I'm focusing out into the skyline, in the middle of which is the Latin America tower with the time blinking from the top in numbers from a digital watch. It must have looked futuristic for about five minutes before becoming charmingly retro. We live in a present of abandoned futures. The rest of the skyline is black blocks and spires against the sun, and clouds dancing with the mountains in pink pastel focus. A sky lit in fuchsia and purple.

The music policy seems to be Eighties, which suits me. 'We Built This City' by Starship comes on and I'm taken back to Her tiny car as we drive somewhere, anywhere, one of the 'adventures' we took. We've decided it's montage music. The local kids are putting on a show to save the Rec Centre. As Starship plays we describe the shots in the montage.

"Two of the kids are looking at the building plans, they're confused - someone walks past, takes the plans, and turns them the right way round. They all nod 'yes'"

"The gang are painting. As each of them turn around we see each of them has a smudge of paint on their face. When we pan to the youngest we see they're covered in paint, everyone shrugs"

"Someone is trying on costumes. Each time they come out, three of the others shake their heads, until we get to the last outfit where everybody nods and gives a thumbs up."

Silly fun, making each other laugh and singing to a stereo that didn't work that well. I smile at the memory and realise it's the first time I've thought about Her and it's done anything other than just hurt.

****

My hostel is by the Zolta - the main square - behind the cathedral. I wake up to the smell of burning sage. Outside, a small man in a dirty shirt and broken baseball cap is making a modest trade from blessing the steady stream of commuters stepping into his chalk circle, and blowing the burning herbs over and around them. Along the planters some hawkers have spread blankets with jewellery, and I can see at least three other people using the sides of the street furniture to throw tarot. Around them. a big stray dog bounces, excited and eager to meet all these new friends. I must pick up my passport today, and I saw an advertisement for a torture museum, so I've decided to find that.

Walking around the torture museum I feel nothing. I mean, the instruments are right there, most of them are the actual objects rather than movie props or modern recreations, so there should be something. Some residual energy. Vibrations of agony that resonate through the ages, auras of pain. But nothing. Without the information cards on the walls this could be an agriculture museum. Death isn't here, and the centuries ago when he was, he was welcomed like a glass of iced water in the desert. Before I go, I stand in front of a steel chair covered in inch-long spikes. The chair would have been slowly heated as the inquisition tried to extract confessions from protestants, forcing them to admit to worshipping the same god in a slightly different way. I'm trying to feel, I don't know, something. I imagine the spikes, the heat, the fear, nothing clicks inside. But then I think of the injustice of it, the Kafkaesque horror of being trapped in that system. The anger and helplessness sticky against my skin and I leave, because I can.

I'm due to pick up my passport. The skyscrapers are glass walls, the occasional foyer an entrance to a world off limits to me. I could be anywhere; New York, Singapore, Sydney, stateless fortresses from nowhere. Wealth is its own country with embassies everywhere. But down the side roads, behind the facades, the cracks show. Broken windows, splashes of graffiti. In the shadows of capitalism's cathedrals are traces of humanity; the dirt, the art, the litter. Compared to the faces and mirrored windows, the tan suits and bellboy uniforms, everybody in the side streets look as if they've all exhaled.

A couple of the smaller skyscrapers are, if not derelict, then unused. Locked up tight, they look dusty, greyed out like an unusable icon on a computer screen. In what was the car park there's a group of 10 or so teenagers using giant reflective windows as a mirror to choreograph a complicated street dance routine. The girl at the front stops and casually pulls up the cut-off jogging bottom legs she's using as leg warmers and waits for me to pass. In much the same way I'm not part of the world of nice suits and air-conditioned cars, I'm not part of their world either. I'm still a ghost with no papers. Picking up the passport I feel no different. No less lost, no more corporal or validated.

I zigzag through the streets, between the two worlds until I find myself on a street of bars. I've wondered into Zona Rosa - one of the centres of nightlife, traditionally bohemian and now home of Mexico city's Gay community. One of these bars has two 12-foot banners with the faded images of the Lady Of Guadalupe and the other of Jesus. Underneath, a phalanx of umbrellas covers the empty smoking area. I can hear live music from inside; what sounds to be a cover of 'Jeremy's Spoken' by Pearl Jam. Inside is ink black, the server pops up from seemingly nowhere, leads me to a low seat by torch, gives me a menu and hovers nearby using the torchlight so I can choose. I order a beer. The stage is small and the singer fills it with his presence. He has a rich rock vocalist voice that easily gets through the nineties alternative the band is focusing on. The low seats make the place seem vaguely Japanese. At the back, the bar serving area has the waiting staff silhouetted against the green neon signs. If I keep my eyes away from that they can adjust to the light - it's pretty full in here especially for early evening, in the corner I can make out a couple necking.

A heavy guy on the table next to me gets my attention, he indicates to two bottles of beer, as if proud of them. I nod in recognition, not sure what response he wanted. The guy puts money on the table, which is immediately snaffled up by a server, shadow melting from the wall. He then hands me both beers as he walks out.

"Gracias" I call after him. I realise he must have bought one of the buckets of beer on offer and only drank six. I love free beer as much as I hate warm beer, so drink the rest of mine and start two new ones fast. Looks like I'm staying awhile, which is no hardship - in the corner of a dive bar with more beer than I strictly need is exactly where I belong.

A new singer replaces the old and starts a set of Mexican rock standards, the crowd knows all the words and I'm people watching. The couple I thought were making out are not at all, the man is literally wrapped around the woman, head down, comforted. A woman arrives in a little black dress, tight, with the hem finishing on her upper thigh. Literally a queue of men forms to hit on her. Even the frontman and guitarist exchange nods and point at her. It's all got a bit hetero in here. I pay my tab.

Night has fallen and the whole area is alight with signs and sounds, promo people half-heartedly are trying to get the dwindling autumn crowd. The night air is still warm and is making my head swim. Everything's close and the pain in my head means I should have eaten something today or it's about to rain. I run down a back street off the strip and nip into the nearest bar. The music is cheesy, the floor is sticky, and a severe looking butch lesbian is DJing between grabbing one of the waitresses that keep swinging by to be grabbed. It's a queer bar, the inhabitants are already messy in their own orbit. The two outward facing walls are big windows smeared with condensation and sin. I hear thunder even over the Latin dance track. The sound cuts through the fog of everyone's excess and relief breaks as the windows pour with water. It's not unlike being in a carwash. I relax a little and I hadn't realised I'd been tense. Maybe I've been unconsciously suppressing the camper aspects of my personality. Being bisexual means I get to 'pass' a lot of the time but Mexico is so macho it seems to leave no room for anything but 100% masculine energy.

It feels late when the bar wraps up. But it's only 11 and I have half a city to cross in sheets of rain with only a woollen jumper as an outer layer. After about 10 minutes my head clears and it coincides with my estimation of the point where my clothes become literally saturated - that is, physically incapable of absorbing any more water. I should be uncomfortable; my clothes are rubbing, my jumper weighs two or three stone more than it should and my socks are squelching. I can hardly see more than half a block in front of me, but I'm laughing: laughing at the sheer relentlessness of the rain, laughing at how I must look to the cars rushing past, and laughing because, although I came looking for Death, I'm cold, dancing in the dirty rain and I feel more alive than I've felt in a long, long while.

This isn't a bad end to my story: died surfing off the coast of Mexico. It's a nice end. As good as I can hope for really. Relax, it's time.

8. That'll Put Dead In Your Pencil

I arrive at the coach station early, having bought my ticket from the counter of the hostel a day ago. It's coming up to the end of October so I want to be out of the city and back in a few days. I chose Porte Escandido almost randomly from the hostel guide, it's a surfing town and I'd realised I hadn't seen the sea since Cancún. It's been a while since I surfed, but what's the worst that can happen?

I pay the taxi driver and he hands me back the coach ticket I'd forgotten I'd given him. Inside, I hand the ticket to a counter clerk who points me to the waiting area. Checking the departure boards there is no bus leaving at the time scheduled, or even going to where I'm booked to go. But I'm early, I wait.

Now, closer to the time, my journey still isn't on the board and looking around I'm the only one with luggage. I've seen bag checking before at stations but no one ever really used them, here it seems everybody does. I go over to the bag checking counter and an incredibly smiley man takes my bag and ticket. The smile falters a little but is quickly back at full beam. He puts up both hands and motions down. Wait here. And he leaves. Minutes later he comes back, still smiling but with a clerk that is not. It's the clerk I showed my ticket to over an hour ago. He indicates I should follow him back to the desk and to bring my bag. I'm confused but I'm not worried, I have my emergency passport, its white, glowing aura radiating protection from any bureaucratic malevolence. At the desk the clerk doesn't speak to me but fetches his supervisor. The clerks behind the large curving desk look young and cabin crew handsome, the supervisor is a little older but looking good for it. He takes my ticket.

"Los solento - I'm sorry this is the wrong station," he says.

"There's more than one?" I'm surprised

"Si, yes" he sympathetically points to a part of the ticket.

"Do I still have time to get there?" It's 45 minutes till departure, the supervisor sags a little.

"No," he says.

"I did ask the taxi driver and showed him my ticket," I say "and I showed that guy my ticket an hour ago," I point to the other clerk. The supervisor clocks his head. Really? And turns on his heel like an angry ballet dancer. He goes over to talk to the clerk. The supervisor points at me, the clerk is averting his eyes but sneaks a look. They talk some more and the supervisor comes back.

"I will give you a new ticket, it will take you near, you can get a bus from there." He taps at the computer and a box spits out a ticket.

"Gracias," I say.

"You're welcome," he says and tells me which departure bay and exactly what time. I check my bag with the smiley baggage guy, he gives me a thumbs up when he checks the ticket. I offer him a tip which he takes backhanded with a round sweep of his arm that ends up in his pocket.

In my neon cocoon I settle in to sleep with my earbuds drifting synthwave keyboards into my head. As the coach moves incrementally around swinging mountain roads, the bus lights flash twice. I'm waiting for the rain, but none comes, outside I can see how close the road is to the edge. Down the valley is a tiny town with its suburbs spreading up the sides of the mountain. We're so far above them already the houses look like models, the tiny Haciendas being lit from inside by fairy lights shining through cardboard windows like somebody sprinkled stars on the tree-lined slopes. The tilt shift effect is made worse by the heavy but perfectly formed grey and black cloud hanging over the town like a special effect. Even that is floating beneath us. I can see from here, at the top of the Sierra Madre del Sur mountains, that the occasional flashes of lighting that crackle underneath it don't just crack down but reach sideways, and even around, to cradle the cloud like thin fingers around a black apple.

****

Next morning, we pull up to a tiny bus station. It has one row of seats, a ticket kiosk next to a bag check, three bus bays and what I think is a shop, judging from the bottles of coke on the counter and the nut display next to it. I buy my ticket from the counter, the lady points to the other bus in the bay - its boarding but from what I can gather from her gesturing to her watch, I don't think it leaves just yet.

Grabbing a water from the shop I go to board the coach. The driver is hanging out at the front by the coach door, I say hello and give him my ticket. He holds up a hand and points to my rucksack, and then the baggage check. I can see the luggage hold of the coach behind him. Grudgingly, I trudge over to the baggage check, a few minutes later the driver steps from the back. He carefully checks my bag in and points over to the coach as if we hadn't just met over there. I walk back to the coach and wait by the door. Seconds later the same driver comes from behind the coach wheeling a massive metal cage with one single piece of luggage in it. Mine.

"Solo un minuto," he shouts as he carefully loads my bag and disappears, wheeling the cage back to the luggage check area. Another minute later he's back; he walks up the corridor between coaches and when he gets to me says "Destino?",

I crack up. Far from offended, I can see him smile too. He doesn't check the ticket, just gestures for me to get on the bus.

****

I find Tower Bridge hostel tucked off the main road. As I enter, a topless man is at the top of a ladder affixing something to the ceiling above a large pool table. I'm handed a cold glass of wheatgrass (to drink, apparently) and someone goes through the paperwork. To the left is a covered seating area consisting of ragged sofa and hammocks that swing over the L-shaped pool that cuts the property in half. The other side of the pool is a bar, seating area and dorm, kitchen and showers. The humped bridge is uneven underfoot and I wonder how many people have fallen in. I ditch my stuff and shower, there are four or five topless men milling about. When I walk to the bar, one of them pops behind the bar to serve me.

Later, I'm drinking by the pool hoping that not wearing a shirt is not compulsory and just some hidden cultural rule I can claim ignorance of, when a woman in her twenties sits nearby working on her laptop. As I'm sitting down again, after buying another beer from one of the SHG's (Shirtless Hot Guys), she looks up.

"Excuse me, where are you from?" she asks.

"England, specifically Birmingham, but I know my accent is all over the shop," I say.

"I'm from Nottingham," she replies.

"Yay Midlanders!" I say.

Hayley is a software engineer and works remotely, so she decided to work around the United States when she met Brandon, who invited her down to Mexico with him. We talk for a while; she's smart and easy to laugh. She gives in and starts drinking too, we toast "Midlands" anytime anyone looks over at us giggling. A large chest-nut-brown man appears from the private rooms upstairs, he wears board shorts and shaggy blonde hair, his broad shoulders and muscle tone all point to a surfer. I peg his age a little older than me. He yawns and spreads his long arms wide, he has the bearing of an older lion surveying his kingdom. He spots Hayley and sits next to her, kissing her deeply in a transparently territorial way.

The beers are three for the price of two, so we quickly fall into rounds. Brandon is a Californian who sold his company before the 2008 crash and now lives on 'his portfolio'. He spends a lot of time travelling. The sun goes down and, despite his size, Brandon's words are slurring and he's missed the table a couple of times on his first attempts at putting the bottle down. He's telling me about cars.

"...of course, I drive a Jeep that drinks gas like… like…" he looks around for inspiration, "beer!"

"Are you not fussed about the environment?" I ask.

"Man, I hate all that bullshit, everyone assumes I'm a democrat because I'm Californian."

"So, you're a Republican?" I ask and glance over at Hayley who rolls her eyes.

"Nah man, but I've got more in common with them than hippies. Take gun control…"

He starts describing the main party line of the Republican party, sprinkled with some neocon libertarianism. To be honest I tune it out, nodding along when polite. Having worked in working-class pubs for more than ten years, I'm more than accustomed to keeping polite conversation going with borderline angry and fragile bigots. I toy with presenting some counter-arguments, but what's the point of riling him further? He's already performing for the SHGs that alternate behind the bar. He swings onto feminism and Hayley bristles.

"…but those bitches never had it so good." he says, there's a beat.

"What?!" says Hayley, incredulously.

"Those uptight feminist bitches, I don't know what they're moaning about, ammiright bud?" He says the last part to me.

"I'm not sticking around if you call women 'bitches'", I say slowly so he can understand through the drink. I can see it rolling around his head. "Will you be okay, Hayley?"

"Fine," she says and briefly touches my leg as I get up to show the frostiness in her reply wasn't for me. I'm hoping it is my presence provoking him and without an audience he can climb down. As I open the door to the dorm ten yards away I can hear Hayley.

"*I'm* a feminist, am *I* a bitch?" she says with a strong accent, and I remember Nottingham was the murder capital of the UK for a while.

"Midlands," I toast.

Next morning the sun is strong, I shower in the basic concrete showers directly behind the bar. I'm a little hungover and fumble for my sunglasses before the rest of my clothes. There's a couple of people about, including the SHGs who may or may not be the same ones from last night, they're playing foosball. I walk to the nearest OXXO and buy a coke for breakfast. When I get back, I sit concentrating on stopping my brain from slipping into a full blown hangover. One of the SHGs comes over.

"What happened last night?" he says.

"What do you mean?"

"I hear you slapped Brandon?"

"What?" I say.

"Someone said you were arguing and you slapped him," the SHG is earnest.

"We argued a little, but I didn't slap him," I say. "But Hayley might have," I add, in my head.

I take my coke and sit next to a guy in a baseball cap, he has a T-shirt on. We nod and he carries on working on a laptop.

"What was that man?" he says.

"Ah nothing, I got into an argument with that big dude, Brad, and now the rumour is that I slapped him," I say.

"Did you?" he asks.

"Nah, I don't really slap people," I say. He takes a long look at me.

"You don't look like a slapper," he says

"Oh, I don't know about that," I laugh. The guy looks confused. "Slapper means something different in England," I add.

Kristian is Canadian and wears a cap backwards without making it look obnoxious. He's warm, despite me distracting him from his work. He does contract work 'for a buddy' and lives and travels in Mexico where the money goes further. A small girl with long, dark hair comes to join us and moves her chair into the sun.

"Hey, did you hear some dude slapped another dude last night at the bar?" she says. I meekly hold my hand up.

"I didn't slap him though, he said some sketchy stuff so I left." I leave out the part about it probably being his girlfriend that slapped him. That seems like their business. Kristian introduces us, his girlfriend's name is Jen and we sit for a while. Jen enjoying the sun, Kristian enjoying his work and me, my headache. Kristian looks up.

"We got company," he says overdramatically, nodding towards the apartments. I bristle. "Don't worry man I've got your back."

"Thank you, that's sweet. But I'm not worried, more embarrassed than anything," I say. Brandon walks past.

"Hey Brandon," I say.

"Hey Buddy," he says, pretending to just notice me now.

"Listen, about last night, no hard feelings? We were both in our cups," I say.

"Oh," he says, seemingly shocked I mentioned it. "Sure, of course, never try and out-drink with the Brits, I reckon."

"Cool, catch you later," I say and go to shake his hand, but remember he's a misogynist so reach for my coke instead. He drifts off to the kitchen.

"That was weird," says Jen looking up from her tan.

"My life is weird," I say.

A little later I head towards the beach, I've not downloaded any maps so make a mental note of the landmarks as I pass. Down the dirt track. Restaurant at the end. Next door to the funeral home. Right. Well not a funeral home, more of a coffin superstore. The retail unit is open, with racks of coffins four or five high. Is that a good omen or a bad omen? This trip to the coast isn't really part of my search for Mr Death but if I find him knocking around here, then all the better. At the bottom of the road is a highway which I cross wearing flip flops, so I might get to meet him sooner than I expect. I don't really know how to get to the beach but beaches are easy to find - you just head downhill and stop just before you get your feet wet.

On the other side of the highway the dirt is churned up mud, hard on the outside but in places brittle, with wet mud underneath. I reach the road heading downwards and pin the fancy bank on the corner onto my mental map as I walk down the hill. It seems I'm on the outskirts of a suburb. I walk past a nice school, walk a bit more and end up back at the same nice school? I take a different path. By now the warm sun has clouded over and the sky is a uniform grey, the air is still light and warm. I see some neon ahead. It's not a rule of mine to head towards neon whenever possible - more of a reflex.

I find myself in a strip of bars and restaurants. They're mostly closed, it being early in the day and late in the season. At the bottom of the road is a small amount of rock leading to a sheer cliff. A little up the wall, the rocks crumble and in a break of the stones somebody has put a laminated postcard of a man carrying a boy on his shoulder. The plastic is loose and the card is crumpled, like it's been wet and dried many times. There are tealight candles scattered in front of it, some dried flowers either side, and the remnants of a knotted rosary which I think used to hang from the corner of the postcard. The picture of course is St Christopher, who is the patron saint of, amongst other things, surfing. But how he got there is a convoluted journey, even for the patron saint of travellers.

Christopher was a big man, belonging to a race of 'giants', the Canaanites. By some accounts he stood seven and a half foot tall, was incredibly strong, and had a 'fearsome face'. Christopher pledged to serve the 'greatest king that ever was', so he travelled until he found a mighty king. In his service to this king he saw the king cross himself at the mention of the Devil. Now Christopher, having a certain type of mind was true to his pledge and so left the king to find the Devil. Soon he found a marauder in the mountains who called himself 'the Devil'. So Christopher set to doing the unsavoury work of serving the marauder. A while later he saw this 'Devil' avoid a roadside cross, so Christopher set off once again to find the king of the cross.

Of course, he didn't find him, but he did find an old man with a white beard, a hermit in fact who taught Christopher how to serve God. Christopher wasn't the type for remembering prayers and fasting made him weak and angry. The hermit suggested he serve God by serving others. Nearby was a fast-moving dangerous river. So Christopher made camp by the side of it helping people across when they needed it. One day, a child waited by the bank and asked for help. Christopher obliged, picking up the child and placing him on his broad shoulders, but the boy was impossibly heavy. It took all of Christopher's strength, and a little bit more than he knew he had, to hold the boy and not get swept away by the strong current. When he set the boy down, he told him how dicey the situation had been.

"I don't think the whole world could have been as heavy as you." The boy smiled and replied,

"You had on your shoulders, not only the whole world but him who made it. I am Christ your King, whom you are serving by this work," and then vanished.

Christopher found himself travelling, talking about his God and comforting Christians who were being martyred by a local king. This king captured Christopher and when he wouldn't sacrifice to the pagan gods the king knew he had to do something about this powerful devout man. One night he sent two women and a basket of jewels to Christopher to buy his loyalty. By the morning the two women left Christopher's care converted to Christianity. The enraged king ordered Christopher executed and, after many attempts, succeeded in beheading him.

St Christopher became the patron saint of travellers and safe passage and, in the early sixties, was adopted by the surfing and hippie culture who, in their most psychedelic expressions, sometimes picked up on him being depicted as a dog headed man. This is from both the icons of Eastern Orthodox Catholicism and Irish medieval tradition, who both describe the race of giants he belonged to as having the face of dogs and eating human flesh.

Who built this mini-shrine in the wall opted for a regular human-faced St Christopher, but I like dog faced St Christopher the best: fiercely loyal and ultimately helpful, and who, like a dog, is capable of great love or terrible acts depending on how he's treated. I tidy up the shrine, prop up the postcard with fresh, sturdier stones, and try and find this beach.

This road is a dead end, so I walk back up and hear a 'hey' from the left of me. It's Jen and one of the SHGs carrying towels. This SHG is a light mocha brown with shaggy, brown hair and long dreads hanging from the back. He has one of those European faces sitting on the borderline of strikingly handsome and boyishly cute.

"Are you going to the beach?" says Jen.

"Yes, well if I can find it," I say.

"Manuel knows the way, come with us," says Jen.

"Sure," says Manuel and we follow. He leads us on a dirt path through a car park and some wasteland whose only main difference is cars.

"Manuel, that's Spanish right?", I ask.

"Yes, I am from Ibiza." His accent is European but not particularly Spanish.

"Aaah a lot of parties, good clubbing too I hear. I've never been," I say.

"English right?" he asks.

"That obvious?"

"Lots of people think Ibiza is a party island, but

there's more to it than that." He's not cross, his face is impassive.

"Of course," I say, "what do you do?"

"I work as a waiter during the party season and I try to travel and surf in the other times," he says.

"You must earn a lot of tips," I say, trying to keep my tongue in my head.

"Yeah, a few, not from the English though." We both laugh. "I live in a cave, so I don't spend a lot, I can save."

"You live in a cave?" I ask. Manuel smiles.

"Sure."

"Isn't that difficult?" I ask. Manuel shrugs.

"You don't care after a little while. I walk to work, they let me charge my phone and shower, we grow some food, always something to do." We stumble out behind some men selling jewellery on a blanket. In front of them is a brick stairwell, the steps are worn and steep. I look away from Manuel and see the Pacific Ocean. The white foam of rapidly breaking waves being the only difference between the sky and sea. The beach is a cove between two rocky cliffs that cup the beach from each side.

The stairs are no joke, steep and seemingly infinite. Not wide enough for two people to pass, but after each flight you're rewarded with a glimpse of the postcard paradise you are a lungful closer to each time. We stop for breath. I notice it's raining a fine mist and judging from my clothes it has been for a while.

"Imagine having to go back up after surfing for a few hours eh?" says Manuel.

The sand is wet and cooling, I'm connected to the world and despite the scenery being straight out of a dream or fantasy, the rain makes everything seem solidly real. Jen and Manuel have gone to hire surfboards. On their way back they ask if I can watch their stuff.

"You sure you'll be okay on your own?" she asks. What a question.

"I'm beginning to think I am," I say. Jen points to the recliners and parasols that line the bottom of the cliff behind us.

"Well, if you want you can sit over there, under cover."

"I'm fine here."

"But it's raining," she says.

"I'm English," I tell her, she seems to understand and runs out into the sea. The sea is some way out, I try to watch them surf but soon they are indistinguishable from the ten or so other surfers in the middle of the cove. Over to the left, rocks bob out of the water near the cliff curve. Three or four surfers are just beyond, risking the rocks to pick up the larger break they ride into the cove. But soon I'm not watching the surfers, distracted by the rhythms of the ocean. The waves seem to be coming in sets of five, with a big wave occasionally between. I've been surfing a few times and the ocean has been my happy place ever since. Floating, tuning yourself to the measure of the waves, being part of something massive, it's like feeling the world breath.

Manuel comes back.

"How was that?" I ask.

"It's rough today - hey can ask a favour?" he says.

"Sure" I say, hoping it's suntan oil related.

"Do you have your phone? Can you take a photo?" he asks, I agree. He takes the surfboard and crunches it nose first into the sand and sits with his back to me facing the ocean. "Get the sea in, the view," he calls out. I take a few and join him on the sand. I show him the pictures and he takes the phone to look closer, he points one out.

"This one, yes?"

I agree.

"May I?" he asks. I don't know what but say yes anyway. He turns and takes a photo of the beach to the left. He then starts swiping and pressing the screen. I really don't want him seeing some of the things I have on there but I'm far too English to tell him to stop. It's deliciously intimate. "I put my number in there so you can send me the photos when we get back." He hands me back my phone. "Thanks man". He holds his hand out for a bro handshake and as we do he comes in for the hug, I'm very aware of the squish of my body and the firmness of his.

"Manuel, el tablero?" we're interrupted by a thin guy in a tatty T-shirt and shorts.

"Si," smiles Manuel, giving him the bro handshake and hug, the man runs off with his board.

"The locals who don't have boards borrow them off the tourists when they're not using them," he explains to me.

We sit watching the surf. From behind us a heavy set local guy with thick dreads comes thundering past, feet slapping solidly on the sand. There's no organised lifeguard, especially this time of year, but the locals who surf here everyday keep an eye out and it's one of those locals who runs past us and hits the waves like a launched ship. We watch as he pulls what could very well be Jen from under a wave. He grabs her board and she clutches it breathing hard. Minutes later, Jen is sitting next to us, draped in our towels, she's still trying to catch her breath and shaking in a way that has nothing to do with the cold.

"I just got caught by a wave and I didn't know which way was up," she says

"It seriously could happen to any of us," I say. We all sit watching the sea, after a while Jen exhales.

"I'm okay," she states. "In fact I'm going back out."

"You sure?" says Manuel.

"Yeah, if I don't go back in now I might never again," she sits for a beat like her brain has sent the signal and she's waiting for her arms and legs to respond. Then she gets up, grabs her board and runs into the surf.

"Wow," I say.

"Wow," Manuel agrees.

"She's hardcore."

"She really is."

"I couldn't do that," I say.

****

The whole hostel is going out - there doesn't seem to be any choice, just a collective decision we're going to a club tonight. Everyone is getting ready and that means different things to different people. The girls are putting make-up on for the first time in weeks, the SHGs are putting on shirts for the first time in weeks, and I'm balancing a beer in the crook of my arm while trying to put eyeliner on in a cracked mirror.

"Starting early?" Kristian asks, seeing my beer.

"Got to be cheaper than wherever we're going," I say.

"Good point," he responds and runs off to get a beer.

"Anyway, I can't drink too much, I've got a surf lesson early tomorrow," I say, when he gets back.

"Is that the same person who Jen used?"

"Yeah, she gave me his number yesterday."

"He's good, you surfed before?" Kristian asks.

"I did a tour of Western Australia, and a handful of times since. It's been a while though, won't hurt to learn from scratch again," I say.

"Yeah good idea," he agrees.

The club is mostly a small bar, with the club part being a multilevel outside area dripping with young, tanned people undulating together. The music is exclusively samba beats. Kristian almost immediately disappears and I'm left with Manuel and the other, now shirted, SHGs. And they like to dance. A lot. They teach me how to dance salsa - it involves wiggling your hips while holding your elbows up and out from the body like you're waiting for your roll-on deodorant to dry. To excuse myself from the dancing I go to the bar. I'm excused a lot.

Later, I'm tired, and honestly, a bit squiffy. I'm taken by a terrible hunger. I slip away without making a big deal out of it. Outside I can make out the bright, sterile lights of an OXXO and I flap towards it, mothlike. Luckily, a mobile hamburger stand greets me first. I'm tucking into my hamburger when a hand claps my back.

"Danny Boy!" it's Kristian. "I was looking for you, me and Jen are gonna get a taxi back, want in?" I realise I can't remember the name of the hostel and had no idea of how I was getting back, or even the general direction of where 'back' was.

"That'd be great man," I say.

"You speak, like, no Spanish right? Like you have no idea what you're eating right now?" he asks.

"It's a burger," I say defensively.

"Do you always order like that?"

"What do you mean?"

"Do you always just hold a finger up and ask for 'one'?" Busted.

"Yeah," I say.

"You know some of these carts sell sheep's brains right?

"...I'll keep away from the ones with skulls on," I say.

"Hey, we should call you 'Juan' from now on," jokes Kristian, guiding me towards the taxi.

****

I wake just before my alarm. I tentatively move my head - not too bad. I'm mildly nauseous but the sea air will soon sort me out. I ache, I've had no real sleep, but I'm passable. I excitedly swing out of bed, stick some of the waterproof Mexican notes in a zip pocket of my board shorts, grab my towel and head to the beach, while the tanned limbs of the rest of the hostel untangle and slowly realise whose bed they've woken up in.

The coffin store at the bottom of the dirt track is now empty. Maybe they had a rush on. I can't decide if this is a good or bad portent.

I meet Will at the top of the steps, he's in his early twenties and dressed only in board shorts despite the solid grey sky and continuous drizzle. He speaks a lot more English than I speak Spanish but that isn't saying much. I follow him downstairs, but a lot slower and my balance is way off. I give myself an honest assessment: I'm a little dizzy, sore from dancing but numb too, and I need a poo. No not numb, drunk. I'm not hungover because I'm still a little bit drunk. When I get downstairs Will is waiting with a board, he lies down on it and pops up on it a few times and invites me to copy. I jump up a couple of times, trying not to fall off the static board. Will holds a finger up, grabs the board and comes back with a much larger one. He lays it down for me to try again and as I lie down I can see it's not a surfboard, it's a windsurfing board.

Will seems, well, not happy, but confident I'm not getting any better. We both grab the huge board to take it to the water. I feel better briefly as the shock of the cold water hits me. I'm on the board paddling while Will swims alongside as easily as a dolphin follows a cruise liner. The waves are getting higher. My arms start to burn from dancing last night. We're in deep water and I'm suddenly not as confident as I was, my head is spinning and I still need that poo. This is a bad idea.

"Will!" I shout and Will swims closer. "Mate, I'm hungover as shit, this is a bad idea."

"You want in?" he says

"Yeah, it's probably wise," I say, Will nods.

"May I take?" he points to the board.

"Now?" I ask. We pause as another wave pushes us in the air and down again.

"Yeah?" he gestures to my ankle cuff. I get in the water and look at the beach, it's about two swimming pool lengths away. I can swim a couple of lengths of a swimming pool. I rip the cuff off and Will shoots off at an impressive clip.

I swim, and swim, and swim. I must be near the beach now. I look up. Nope, actually I don't seem to be any closer to the beach at all. Shit. I float. The sea sucks shallow and then swells lifting me up. Okay. Swim hard.

So I swim hard, until my arms burn and my legs are weirdly loose. I've got to be close to the beach now.

No.

This isn't funny now. The white grip of panic just at the edge of my headache. I look around for Will, he's gone. No one is here. I'm alone. And scared. I take a deep breath and float on my back. My heart is thumping from exertion and fear. My arms are beyond sore. Suddenly, I'm under water. I take a mouthful as my head breaks the surface again and I panic swim, while coughing. I'm thrashing more than anything. My breathing is more occupied with trying to cough up the water my nose keeps inhaling. And, when I can see it, the beach is as far away as ever. This is it. I can't do this

As endings go, this isn't a bad one. The thought is flat and calm. I'm choking and flailing, and it's surrounded by panic and pain. But it's there and clear.

I'm okay with this.

But. But if I am going to die, I'm going to die swimming. I realise now this thought isn't brave or tough. I just decided I wanted to pass out and drown rather than be conscious while my lungs fill with cold sea water. I put my head down and swim, being ready for it to be literally the last thing I do.

I swim, past pain, past everything.

I look up and I'm actually near the beach. I see Will 50 metres away, he gestures for me to stand, I'm shocked to be so close and put my feet down. And I'm completely submerged. I look up, I'm at least six feet under the surface. Twat. But I'm close. I push up, gulp air and tell my legs to swim before they tell me they can't.

Sand. My legs feel sand before my arms, and I'm crawling. And then I'm not. My limbs have given way. Someone is tapping my hand. I look up at one of the locals who is gesturing for me to move up the beach, pointing to the waves creeping up my legs. I crawl a little further. The local has joined the others with a shrug, I can't feel anything. The black at the edge of my vision is slowly growing until the world is a small white point far away in front of me. I know passing out would feel so good right now, but I fight the blackness. If I pass out now I will definitely shit myself in front of the locals.

Half crawling, half stumbling I make it to the sun loungers, there's a woman setting up her bar shed for the day. The blackness is creeping back.

"Toilet? Toilet? Errrm BANOS!" I say. She says something about money.

"After after after" I shout and gesture. My voice isn't a shout, it's a hoarse rasp. She gives me a key and points to the portaloos. My numb hands grab the padlock and it opens without the key. I barely get my shorts down before it happens.

And then I wake up on the toilet. I've never been so tired, my body is heavy like trying to run in a dream. I land heavily into a lounger, I can barely see. The only thing I can feel is the rain on my skin. The lady is close. I hold the money I got from my shorts pocket out.

"Aqua" I think I whisper before I stop fighting it and pass out.

When I come round the bar lady has set the water in front of me and closed my unconscious hand around the change. I can't move. 'I live here now' I think before I pass out again.

I wake up again to the sound of flat drumming, the rain hitting the parasol like a Slipknot solo. Someone must have put the umbrella over me when the rain got heavy. My legs are fire and my arms are worse. I've drank most of the water in front of me, I have no real memory of doing it, but I know it was me because my throat isn't as rough as before. The sea is churning as if it's trying to fight the rain. I try and summon some sort of feeling about it - anger, fear - but I can't. My brain is numb and so are my toes. I could rest some more but my arms and legs are only going to get worse. It's best to get to my bunk with my little bag of lotions, downers, and opiates. Plus, if there's something shitty I have to do I just want to get it over with, even if it's climbing several thousand flights of steep slick stairs.

The rain hits me in lazy, fat spots and I'm low key surprised when it doesn't taste like salt. I do notice, with a laugh, I'm completely hangover free.

Seconds after I'm out of my wet clothes I'm asleep in my bunk.

Thunder cracks and jolts me awake; it sounds like it happened metres away. It's nighttime, but there are people out by the bar. Normally you'd be able to pick out their conversations over the music but the lashing tropical rain reduces all other noise to the background. Being inside while it's raining, especially after drying off, is a universal comforting feeling, but in that bed it's more than that. I'm anointed, dry, safe. I'm alive I think, no joy to that thought, no achievement. Nothing but a solid statement of fact. I'm alive… and as the thunder and flashes soothe me asleep again… so now what?

The storm's sticking around. I don't really feel like company, so I fake a stomach bug and stay in my bunk reading. Every so often a lightning strike takes the power out for a while; we hear a crack, the lights dim, and everybody cheers, even me from my bed. On a trip to the toilet I see the SHGs by the pool enjoying the rain. I walk past Manuel in a hammock, he raises his smoothie.

"Trapped in paradise," he says.

The dog is warm and has found a spot on the sofa with no springs, so anywhere you sit gravity rolls you closer to her. She's a street dog, one of the many you see in Mexico, indeterminate of breed, or age. Even the colour is hard to pin down, kind of a sandy brown. She looks clean, well fed even, and her fur is soft. She shifts slightly when I start to stroke her so I can better get at a spot between her shoulder blades she seems to prefer. I'm probing the memory of nearly drowning with my mind tongue, constantly bothering my brain's loose tooth.

One of the upsetting things is the thought of not being able to surf again, although even thinking about it right now sends my stomach into a cold flip. It's silly, but one of the alternative futures to the one I lost with Her was being an old surf crusty, living in a van, driving the coast looking for waves. But as it is now, that future, like many others, is as dead as I nearly was. The dog looks around as if I had the temerity to stop the fuss to wipe the tears from my face.

"Alright, alright," I placate and get back to stroking. Of course there are futures I don't want dying all the time. There is a future where I didn't make it: I pass out, and wake up taking a panic breath, taking in cold salt water, brain screaming to kick, breath, to live. Again, my stomach flips imagining it. Then what? Will phoning the police, the hostel, then someone making the call to my mom. I can see my mom at the other end of the call. It's awful, but the relief when I snap out of that reverie is a warm flush, cozy, like a shot of morphine or a warm dog on a wet day. The dog looks round. She knows I'll be okay and at that moment I know it too.

Next afternoon Jen and Kristian leave, I'm booking my bus for the next day when the storm breaks.

"Where did you get that?" It's the manager, she's my age with long blonde hair and a Nordic edge to her accented English. She's pointing towards the pizza I walked down the road to get.

"The place down the road."

"Is it good?" she asks.

"Spectacularly bad actually, try it," she takes a slice.

"May I?" she asks pointing to a seat.

"Of course, your gaff," I say. She sits.

"It's just… you haven't been out of your bunk in a while." She's making it sound casual but I know it's the reason she's over here.

"I know, stomach bug," I say.

"Okay" she says.

"And honestly? I haven't had the energy for being around people, you know?"

"But you're feeling better now?" she asks, as she takes a bite out of the pizza. "Wow, that is cardboard."

"I know, it tastes like it's been printed rather than cooked," I agree.

"You should eat the box instead." Lena is the manager's name, the European I hear in her accent is German but she travels a lot. She balances the kindness in her tone with a gentle authority. She gets herself wine from the bar and me a beer. I ask her how she came here, she tells me she chose it because of its name.

"Puerto Escondido means hidden port, it sounded so mysterious. How could I not go to The Hidden Port? So evocative." She brushes her hair from her face and peers at me through her big manga eyes. "And when I found out how it got its name, I had to come."

"How did it get its name?" I ask.

"The story goes, when the pirate brothers Andre and Francis Drake split up, Andre…"

"Hang on, Francis Drake wasn't a pirate," I interrupt. She laughs.

"Only to the English, to everyone else he was known as 'El Draco' The Dragon."

"Oh."

"Well, his brother had captured a native woman further up the coast. When he laid anchor here the woman escaped his cabin, swam to shore, and hid in the thorn bushes," Lena takes a sip of her wine. "The pirates searched and searched but didn't find her, and every time they passed this way they would come ashore and look again. But they never found her." Lena smiles to herself in satisfaction.

Passing out feels good, one second everything
hurts, your legs burn, your lungs are tired
and muscles you didn't know you even had
in your back are screaming for attention.
The next second it's gone. Nothing but the
black. Nothing, but the feeling that someone
is standing behind you. Do you dream when
you're unconscious? A hand, a comforting hand.
A phrase from a long forgotten English class
floats 'Time's wingèd chariot hurrying near'.

9. You Look Like Death

My last journey by Mexican coach, and I think to myself as I settle into my usual seat, the easiest yet. The first and last trip with nothing to worry about. I have my passport and the coach terminates at Mexico City, so I don't even have to stay awake to check each stop. No changes to worry about, no checking the street signs as they go past wondering if this is where I should be getting off. 'I can sleep the whole journey if I want to,' I think, as I wind the strap of my bag around my leg and settle in to sleep.

The bus pulling into a sharp stop wakes me up. The clock at the front reads a little after three in the morning. We're pulling up at a checkpoint on a freeway somewhere, the overhead lights click on and a man in blue fatigues and a beret gets on the coach. Under his arm swings a machine gun of some kind. He shouts something and everyone starts getting their tickets and driving licences out. I pull out my bus ticket and my passport and hold it up for inspection. He walks along the coach aisle nodding at each one once he's done. He pauses at mine, looks at me, looks at the passport. He says something in Spanish.

"Lo soloento, no habla Espanol," I say. He takes the passport off me and speaks again, more sternly this time. I go to repeat "I don't speak Spanish," but I don't even get to "lo soloento," before he turns and walks away with my passport, making a small gesture which I take to mean "follow me". I briefly panic. Do I grab my bag, with my wallet and everything in it? Or will taking it make him more inclined to keep me off the coach? I chance it and grab it following him. The traffic outside is still pretty regular for three in the morning, its cold and the air is thick with exhaust. He leads me to a pair of guards identical in uniform, they casually arrange themselves either side of me while raising their threat awareness levels from 1 to 1.00000001. The man with my passport has got back on the coach. We wait. As he steps off again the coach doors close with a pppppppsht, and the coach pulls off. My blood goes cold. He walks over and speaks Spanish at me again, but I can barely take in what's going on as I watch the coach pull away and, thankfully, pull in at the lay by a little bit further up, hopefully waiting for me. The official with my passport has disappeared. Me and my two guard friends stand in the cold smog. I smile weakly at one; it is not returned. My hand creeps to my wallet and discreetly gets out some paper money to 'pay the fine'.

Soon, the trooper is back with another man in a near identical uniform - except the badges, the shade of his beret, and the swing of his shoulders all scream 'in charge'. He has my emergency passport in one hand and he's hitting it with the back of his free hand as he speaks to me.

"Stamp, where is stamp?"

"It's not stamped yet, it's an emergency passport. The stamped one was stolen."

"Then visa, where is visa?" he counters.

"It was stolen at the same time, I was told I should get it on the way out, at the airport."

"When did you enter the country?" he asks. I honestly

can't remember the date, or even remember any date.

"September 11th," I pluck from nowhere and realise what I just said. He hands me my passport and jabs at it with big fingers.

"You need visa," he says.

"I'll get one," I assure him. Pssssht. The coach has just let off its airbrakes, I pray it's not going without me.

"Okay get visa." he says, and with a nod the guards take half a step away.

"I can go?"

"Go," he nods. I run to the coach and bang on the door, the driver looks surprised to see me but he lets me on and pulls off quickly before I get to my seat.

****

As I discovered, there is more than one coach station in Mexico City, and I learn as the coach pulls in that I had already been to the nice one. Not that there's anything wrong with this one, it's just a little used, built in the seventies and not updated since is my guess. The pre-booked taxi booth is manned by a lady with big, framed glasses. She smiles at me as I hand over my hostel's address. She gives me a ticket with a price on and I hand her a note out of my pocket. She laughs, says something and hands it back. It must not be enough, so I hand her a different note with the first. She's laughing and talking a lot. She pushes both notes under the perspex. I take them back and inspect them, maybe they're damaged? The face of Gandhi looks up and, from the other, a church from a Hungarian Kroner. I have a pocket in my wallet with money left over from other trips. These are the notes my fingers found when looking for bribe money. I wonder how the officials would have reacted at the offer of a few hundred rupees and enough Kroner to buy a newspaper. The woman behind the counter is laughing even harder at my face as I realise what I'd been doing. I pay the lady with real money and jump into the taxi.

It's afternoon by the time I get to the hostel. We pull up outside an old art deco hotel on the corner of a six-lane intersection, the shops around it are shuttered or under scaffolding, all of it stratified with layers of poster, graffiti, and grime. A bouncer stands by the door, a visual echo of the doormen and that would have stood here in its heyday, directing the bellboys as the great and the beautiful glide in. I'm early for check in but they take my rucksack and allow me in the bar foyer area. It's furnished with painstaking eclecticness, a couple of large tables in the middle, with smaller tables, couches and even a few chaise lounges. It's modern and busy. Maybe 'busy' is the wrong word. It's populous, but sedate - mostly people staring intently at laptops, except one table where some people are one half of a thoroughly professional Skype call. These will be the Digital Nomads the hostel website mentioned, people like Kristian and Hayley who work remotely and use that freedom to travel, normally to places where the money they earn goes much further. On one of the chaise lounges a real backpacker snores loudly over his rucksack.

****

The downstairs work area has been cleared for a dance floor. It's empty, so is the bar. The bar man is looking dutifully busy despite having nothing to do.

"Rushed off your feet then?" I say. He smiles and gestures over to the corner where a solitary DJ is mixing music for no-one.

"It's him I feel sorry for," he says.

"That's kinda sad."

"Then go dance," the bartender goads.

"Okay, it's not that sad," I say, and he laughs

"What can I get you?"

"I was told I'd get a free drink, this is the Tuesday new arrivals party thing right?" I say.

"Yep, you arrive this week?" he asks.

"Today actually." He hands me a Heineken and I stay at the bar to drink it. The DJ drops a track and looks up to see if anybody reacts, I accidentally catch his eye so do a nod of encouragement, he seems disappointed and I understand. I finish the Heineken and, as I place the bottle back on the bar, the barman hands me a fresh one. I go to pay.

"Don't worry about it," he says.

"You sure?"

"There's some set aside for the night," he says.

"Yeah, but surely you drink the leftover ones right? I

don't want to drink your stash." He gives a small nod and points towards where he was cleaning earlier - discreetly behind the glasses is half a bottle of Heineken. "Then thank you," I say leaning on the 'you'.

I leave the hostel in search of people. A few blocks away, behind a giant sand coloured building with high walls that looks more like a fort than the university it apparently is, I find a street of small bars. I pick the busiest looking. It looks like an Italian bistro crossed with an early Rauschenberg/Warhol collaboration. The walls are an orgy of packaging, found objects and framed prints in unlikely juxtaposition, smeared with thick impasto paint and covered in layers of graffiti. I settle in and order a beer as the song *Linger* by the Cranberries comes on. It's a song I've never taken seriously before even though it came out in that sweet spot in my teens where every song you hear is permanently wired into your taste glands. But now, half a beer in, I'm singing along and it's like a warm bath of nostalgia.

It's all couples in here. The oldest pair, in their fifties, are kissing constantly. One couple leaves, their toddler is being stubborn and decides to stay. The parents make a big show of leaving him, expecting him to realise they're gone and immediately follow them out, but the kid, either sensing their ruse or simply not giving a fuck, is made of sterner stuff and pulls his seat closer to the table. The parents, really selling the leaving thing have gone and I'm the only one in sight watching this child. Just as I'm getting used to being a parent, the real ones come back and have a sterner word, now backed up by a waiter who is gamely playing bad cop. The parents leave again but again the child is having none of it. He seems committed to living at a bar until he buries his face in the seat and starts to cry. Two men walk in and head over to what they think is an empty table and really couldn't be more confused to find a toddler unattended, slumped over the table like a drunk ghost. They sit at the table and, I suppose, get used to their new lives with a three year old, absolving me once again of that burden. The parents, defeated, return for the child and with no negotiation this time, pick him up. The child's defence is spirited, wrapping his arms around a chair leg shouting 'no!'. The two men sit there, I expect quietly praying the couple manhandling the child are, in fact, its parents.

The music has been solidly power ballads for a while. Currently it's Simple Minds' 'Don't You Forget About Me'. I make a game of trying to guess the next song. I think 'Nothing's Going To Stop Us Now' or 'Africa', at the crunch I go for 'Africa'. It's not, but after that the familiar strains of 'Africa' comes on, and after that 'Nothing's Going To Stop Us Now'. No one celebrates, which shouldn't be surprising because it's a game I've played entirely in my own head against no one.

According to the type of Instagram post that has a photo of some nice trees and a quirky font, the word 'sondar' describes the experience of realising that everyone you walk past and encounter has as rich and complex interior as you do. And in a bar halfway across the world, watching couples flirt and touch, discuss and divulge, It's a useful word to know. When travelling, your memories can fade quickly, only leaving you with the most vivid. A gladiatorial fight of bright colours and smells and feelings. Unfortunately, a sense of contentment and acceptance is a weak fighter, a malnourished slave boy against a lion. But I'm rooting for this guy, this humble feeling of perspective and belonging that comes four beers deep, and the sondar of knowing you're an extra in someone else's movie, an easter egg only the most obsessive fan would get.

A waiter is placing food in front of the man next to me, I look over at the movement and make eye contact, he's American which is a fair assumption. He wears a supreme branded camo hat on top of big hair that frizzes out of the sides, over a blue shirt he has a bum-bag holstered around one shoulder and brightly coloured Hawaiian shorts. He looks like a cult leader on a package holiday. He gestures to the food and tells me,

"I think 'vegetarian' and 'tacos' are a contradiction, but here goes," and proceeds to demolish them in minutes. I nod.

"Here I Go Again On My Own" I say, still playing the game reflexively.

"Nah man, this is 'Love Is A Battlefield' by Deborah Harry," he corrects.

"I think it's Pat Benatar, and I was guessing the next one, it's a game I'm playing."

"Oh, got any right so far?" he says.

"Close," I shrug. Johnny invites me to join him as the waitress comes to take the plate away. He asks if I've ever had mezcal "the good stuff," he insists. I admit I haven't, the waitress waits for the drinks order. Johnny orders for both of us, I think it's going to be a string of complicated Spanish but Johnny smiles at the waitress.

"Two mezcal, the same as I had the other night," he holds up two fingers so she knows 'two'. The mezcal comes in glasses slightly bigger than shot glasses with red powder around the rim. They're served with a small plate of lime quarters sprinkled with the same red powder.

"Do we shoot it?" I ask.

"Nah man, savour it and then suck on the fruit," he says, and demonstrates. I do the same. The mezcal is deep and both earthy and fruity at the same time, this is mirrored by the lime; sweet and sharp with the salty powder adding a savoury texture too.

"That's delicious," I say "what's the red stuff?"

"Kayleigh," shouts Johnny. The volume in which we shout our guesses has risen the more we play the game. "The red stuff?" he asks.

"Yeah," I say, taking a longer sip of the mezcal and suck of powdery lime.

"Worm salt," he says, checking for a reaction.

"Worm salt?" I say.

"Yeah it's chili, salt and crushed worm, the same worm from the bottles of tequila you can get."

"No shit?" I ask.

"No shit," he confirms. I look at the lime in my hand and take a suck. The next song isn't 'Kayleigh' nor the next. We haven't been correct once but we still guess and we've been close a couple of times. We have several more mezcals with God knows how many crushed worms. Johnny tells me he was here to visit a girlfriend up by the border but they split up so he's meeting his other girlfriend in the city tomorrow. The music changes abruptly from power ballads to Italian folk music, which isn't a million miles away from Spanish folk music to my ears. I tell Johnny I'm here to find Death because I've got some questions to ask.

"What questions?" asks Johnny.

"Oh you know 'why?' that sort of thing," I say.

"Why what?"

"Why is it set up like it is? Why is it so fucking unfair?" I surprise myself by being a little teary on the last part. Johnny pauses.

"Why do you think he's going to know? How do you know he's not just some middleman on commission?" he asks.

"Don't know till I find him" I say. Johnny doesn't answer, just holds his glass up for a toast. We hit glasses and suck down more insect dust. A song starts, it's in Italian but it's familiar, like it's been on an advert or something.

"I recognise this, is this Elvis or something?" I ask.

"Nah, I think Elvis did a version. My dad's Italian, this is a guy called Mario Lanza, have you heard of him?"

"My nan loved him," I say.

"My nan too," we toast again.

"What's it called?" I ask.

"Santa Lucia," says Johnny.

****

Mezcal and worm salt hangovers are fine - a manageable low level of pain and nausea which is constant and unchanging like a drum machine track. Pushing on my sunglasses with the same intensity as most people affix the overhead masks that drop down on a plane, I leave the hostel into the low autumn sun. Next door is a little newsagent and I pop into to buy the Mexican Coke my neurons have screamed for from the moment I wake up every morning. I could give up anytime I wanted, I swear. As the man behind the counter is making my change his hand lingers for a second. I look up.

"You like rock." It's not a question, and it's not an accusation I could deny, covered in tattoos and piercings.

"Huh?" I grunt. I understand what he said, just not why. He says it again, this time strumming a tiny and imaginary guitar. I can't help but join him in smiling.

"Sure," I say, he nods and points to next door.

"You go."

"Err okay, will do," I give him a thumbs up as I leave. Next door is an entrance to what looks like flats - just shared stairs, stone painted white. I've walked past a few times and there has been the occasional scene punk or greebo outside smoking a cigarette. Poking my head in today, there doesn't seem to be a shop or tattoo parlour in there, if anything it seems even more residential. I'll check it out later; sometimes the gigs that aren't meant to be there are the best ones

****

Smoke is billowing from the crushed cigarette on the empty dance floor. Beside it a long and pointed foot is twisting in time with rock and roll music. It's jarring to see cigarettes indoors and I'm trying to remember if the no smoking indoors rule has made it over here to Venice yet. Of course, even if it had the gig we're waiting for is in what looks like an abandoned restaurant and is being run by the first people I've seen all weekend who's scarves didn't cost more than my entire outfit. I've been to a few illegal raves in my dancing days and this looks very much like every one I've ever been too. Warm beer served in plastic cups and hasty graffiti covering the numerous health and safety violations. Dirty floors and furniture found on the side of the road. Toilet facilities that start bad and degenerate over the night. All these are pleasingly familiar and more so to know that these markers cross borders.

There is one punk behind the hole in the wall serving as a makeshift bar who seems too stoned to figure out how money works. But that's fine as most people seem to have brought their own drinks anyway.

Zona Bandita is on a backstreet, hidden by the bus station. The entrance is no more than a wooden shed door. We arrive at the time we saw advertised on the photocopy I pulled off a pillar while sightseeing - 11pm. We see, perhaps, three people at the bottom of a path and decide to go for a drink until it's a little less sketchy. There is literally nowhere else open, so we spend an hour wandering down alleys and side-streets, of which Venice is blessed with an abundance. An hour later we return. The place isn't exactly jumping but there is music, so we give a man with a beard five Euros and walk in. One of the most interesting things about travelling is not only learning the similarities, but also learning the differences, customs and cultures of other places. Tonight we learn that, in Venice, if a gig is advertised to start at 11, only tourists turn up before one.

The music is rock and roll. Not the abstract rock and roll that most guitar-based bands use as an ideology and excuse to throw bar stools at groupies, but actual Rock and Fucking Roll, the music that invented the teenager. Switch blade steel guitars, 4:4 heartbeat time and Brylcream hair. It's ace. The DJ's and, a little later, the bands, are wearing tight, sharp suits, slicked down parted hair, and everyone sports some sort of trimmed facial hair.

Somehow, the DJs signal that the gig is about to start without moving, speaking or stopping the music and the room goes from ten to a hundred people and a lot of smoke. The first band is a two-piece called Wildmen. It's a lucky break for them that the makeshift stage has just enough room for both members. I'm always happy to see a singing drummer, although, for most, Phil Collins probably shat in that shower for good in the eighties. They describe themselves as 'garage blues' on the flyer, 'garage' seemingly being Italian for 'screaming passion'. Any two-piece with guitar and drummer are going to be compared with the White Stripes, but in this case the Wildmen stand-up to that comparison delivering stripped down bluesy rock and roll that occasionally bubbles into breakneck guitar and fast driven thumping drums. The crowd don't applaud between songs but rather stand baffled like participants in a musical hit and run.

Then, there is a hassle of leads, people and steel - the sort of hassle that can only come from trying to fit a six-piece band on a stage that struggled with two. Just as the crowd start drifting away, the front man of Vomit Tongues throws his mic into the air, catches it with a flourish and a guttural scream kicks off a sound that is somewhere between early punk and diet-pill speed rock and roll. The performance is a blur interspersed with gaps so the guitarists can retune their guitars and plug the leads back in. Some would point out that this could be overcome by not smashing the necks of their guitars against the cymbals, crowd surfing and spitting at each other. But fuck those people, they know nothing of Rock and Fucking Roll.

These gaps are odd, but give the now dancing, bouncing crowd a breather. When the songs finish the band go from being Dionysian infused raw nerves, screaming personifications of our unconscious passion of life, and go back to being shuffling awkward young men. Then, with a rebel yell and a slam on the bass drum they're back to being avatars of abandon.

****

I first figured out how to use a subway on the Paris Metro on a school trip as a teenager. I remember the moment - staring at the map and signs and a sudden shift, and it all made sense. After that, over a couple of summers spent on the east coast of America I cemented this knowledge flinging myself around New York on the subway. Now whenever I'm in London, I'm completely comfortable using the tube. Or Berlin, or Sydney, or Prague. That's the thing I love about them, it's a uniquely urban transferable skill, separate from language or cultural familiarity.

Mexico City's subway - or STC - was built in the late sixties and a lot of it still has that retro modern feel. Concrete and orange tile, curved edges, and fluorescent lights behind scratched perspex. When it was first built the literacy rate in the city was somewhere around 35% so every station has a name but also a logo. The signage makes clear logical sense without the words - for example, every line has a colour. The stations will use that colour of the line except if they are a connection, then they will split the sign diagonally with the colours of the connecting line.

Once downstairs, you find the booth selling tickets. I'd been told you just hand them the money and they give you the equivalent in tickets, you only need to specify if you hand them a note. The woman at the booth is efficient. The price is a flat fee of five pesos (about 20p) which makes it one of the cheapest in the world. I hand over a 10 peso coin. She swipes the money away and hands me the stiff cardboard tickets in a practiced glide. I find my platform and it's busy; lots of people standing far closer together than is comfortable for someone with an English sense of personal space. The train comes and is too full, but the doors open and the crowd squeezes in. I'm filtered to the front but hang back not wanting to push myself into a clearly full carriage. I'm still on the platform when the doors close. No problem. I'll catch the next one. My hangover, somewhat improved by the coke earlier, winces at the thought of being near so many people. I have to sooth it like a nervous pet. The next train comes, again full. The doors open and because the platform has built up behind me, the crowd pushes me into the car where we're literally squished together. I can't reach any of the poles or straps so my fingers grip the fan duct above me. Now, I'm the average size for an English guy, which is a foot taller than most Mexicans, this means their noses fit almost snugly into my exposed armpit. After one station I realise the exercise of trying to hold on is pointless anyway - the tightly packed mass of people keep each other standing because there is simply no room to fall.

Luckily, the majority of the crowd are going to the same place as I am and we are spewed out at the Zoloto. I find a place to stand with a good view of the parade route and settle in. I am, as ever, early. This is the historic Día de los Muertos Parade of Mexico City, years of tradition and culture right? Well, no. The first parade happened somewhere in 2014 as part of a massive set piece for the filming of the 2015 James Bond film 'SPECTRE'. After the film was released the Mexican tourist board was inundated by people asking when the parade was each year and, as surly supply meets demand, Mexico City had its first Días De los Muertos Parade in 2016. In fact, the event I'm attending today will be its only third real parade. The spot where I've settled is actually in the James Bond sequence briefly. To the side of one of the council buildings is an arched walkway the end of which is barriered off, but it gives me a perfect view of the street. The parade doesn't end in the main square like the film but rather uses two sides of it in the middle of the route.

I've been here a while and there are perhaps two families next to me, which is weird because all around me the crowd is already two or three people deep. I look back and the police have taped off the building - they must have done this shortly after I arrived and decided not to make us move. I can see a woman with a pram and a thoroughly embarrassed husband, arguing with the officer to be let in. She keeps gesturing over at us. It starts to rain, taking most of the crowd by surprise - one of those summer showers that come from almost nowhere. The parade was now due to start an hour ago and I'm beginning not to feel great about being penned into anywhere by the police.

The rain stops and I decide to ignore the sunk cost fallacy that is keeping me here. I walk over to the barrier. The two police officers see me coming and make no attempt to open it. Ignorance is my shield and foreignness is my sword. I prepare "I'm deeply sorry officer". I'll start, "I had no idea I wasn't supposed to be there, nobody said a thing to me," and then I'll Hugh Grant a bumbling handshake, "Well, things to do," and I'll raise my hat, because in this imaginary scenario I'm wearing a bowler hat and, fuck it, a monocle too. What I actually do is approach the barrier without directly looking at the police officers and, when I can see it can't be undone, belly vault it and walk away waiting for the shout for me to stop. The imaginary bowler hatted version of me drops his monocle in disgust "Coward," he spits.

I find a place to pee and decide to give the parade another go. All the posters say it starts at 12 but it's now closer to three so I push into the main square to see if I can get a decent spot. I find a place that's four deep from the barriers, but mostly smaller people. I decide to give it half an hour more before cutting my losses.

Two hours later I'm still standing. It's as packed as the subway. About an hour ago I looked around and was faced with a swimming pool's worth of people tightly squoze together; to get out would involve over half an hour of pushing and apologising. It's weird to feel claustrophobic but still able to see the sky, but anyone who has been in a crowd of this size will know. At this point the crowd stops being individuals; it becomes this living, heaving thing. When somebody moves it becomes a ripple. Every so often a sanitation guy pushes his cart along the route, the mass cheers and claps and whistles at the poor fella, but this causes an undulation as those at the back push forward thinking the parade has started. The teenage girls next to me have linked arms to stop themselves being ebbed away. The guy just in front has his arms around his girlfriend, elbows out, giving her half an inch clearance around herself. A woman with her friends has taken to watching a Spanish TV show, and around her everyone is making eye contact and rolling their eyes.

The sky darkened a while ago and the mass undulates anew whenever the rain starts falling as they put on their raincoats or pull open their umbrellas. The linked-arms girls put up a brolly, and after a minute of having the spokes jabbed near his eyes the stranger behind them takes it and holds it above all of their heads. The family next to the barriers have sent their two youngest over the barriers to sit in the road, the banner on the barrier flipped over and used as a tent. The security staff who have been ushering people out of the road for the last couple of hours pointedly not seeing them. I scan the crowd's faces for Death. The situation is precarious: one firework, misplaced word, or loud noise could turn this situation into a tragedy. Surely, he'd be here? Maybe he found a better view.

The parade finally comes into view prompting another eddy of the mass as everybody gets their phones out at once. We hear it first; samba drumming, whistles and cheers. There are floating turtles and whales as big as medium-sized cars overhead, being wrestled by teams of rope pullers. The turtles' backs are a bright kaleidoscope of colours while their bellies are painted with the stark black and white representations of their skeletons.

The floats are a depiction of the history of Mexico. We get marching Aztec warriors, Mayan priests, Spanish galleons and a steamer adorned with flappers, all painted with skull faces. A troupe of dancers with large butterfly wings spin and twirl. They never stop or betray the hours they have probably been dancing, each flap and spin as light as the last. The monarch butterfly was important to the Aztec, they believed them to be the carriers of souls of warriors dead from battle and, possibly because of their migration patterns, the souls of children who come back to visit on the Day of the Dead.

A giant skeleton torso rolls past in a wide brimmed hat and colourful flowers, her long boney arms bounce and lurch like she wants to grab the crowd. This is Las Calavera Catrina, roughly translated as 'well-dressed skull woman'. Today she has come to be a symbol of affection for the Mexican people, a homage to their tendency to laugh and celebrate death. She is now one of the most ubiquitous images associated with the festival. Sometimes it's hard to pin down the origin of folk images and traditions but La Catrine can be traced

back to a single etching in a news pamphlet. The image
was originally mocking the garbancera - a nickname
for native people that copied European dress and styles.
Now she's everywhere. The parade is on Saturday,
four days before Día de los Muertos starts properly, but
already she's in shop windows, posters, and the paper
decorations appearing in windows.

After the last marching band, the crowd turns at once
and faces itself for the first time. I could push my way
through but to get to where? Everybody wants to be out
of the crowd while simultaneously being part of it. I'm
panicked briefly. Something about being helpless has put
me back in the ocean, treading water as the waves rock
me from all sides.

****

Buying beers and sitting in the kitchen is universal
backpacker code for 'lets get fucked up and do
something we'll regret', but I'm two beers along and
the only action here is a group of ten who have clubbed
together for a potluck that consists mainly of vegan
stir fry and smiling for too long. They are all at least
ten years younger than me and diverse enough to be a
fucking Pringles commercial. I'm itchy to go out, the city
is gearing up for a big night - it's the Saturday closest to
Halloween so while the decorations aren't quite everywhere yet, the bars and clubs have been flyering and
flyposting hard. There is an energy in the air outside

and I'm missing it sitting in a well-appointed kitchen with the Stepford nomads.

On my way out of the door I notice there's an altar for the Day of the Dead on the other side of the dancefloor. There's nothing more self-consciousness inducing than crossing an empty dance floor. Zen Buddhists should go to crap discos for enlightenment. The altar is a table with two levels covered in a bright orange cloth, on it have been placed photographs - a man in speedos and a guitar - the picture looks old, like it was taken in the seventies. And the other is a teenager sitting on a scooter, pride puffing his chest and grinning out of his eyes. The sides of the altar are decorated with round orange flowers, freshly cut. There's a large jug of water, a bowl of salt, open bottles of Corona, fresh fruit and candles in jam jars, which in the harsh lights of the 'club' give the altar a warm otherworldly glow. A sign on an adjacency table reads "Dias De Los Accidentados - today we remember those that died from accidents".

I think about today, unsafe in a crowd for the first time in my life, and suppress a shudder. I take a moment, not for anyone specifically but just to add my love and reverence to the altar and the people who may be struggling today.

The entrance of the place I was pointed to by the newsagent is crowded with people smoking and chatting, there's undefinable music coming from up the stairs. There is a me that at one time wouldn't have gone up those stairs, a me that would have used fictional 'bad vibes' to explain why. But that me is gone, like a lot of mes, I suppose we die all the time shedding personalities like snakeskin against rough rocks.

The stairs get more scrawled upon as I climb. It's four flights up before I meet a gaggle of people by an open door, they're spilling about and laughing but one of them has a small lockbox so I hand her a note and accept the hand stamp and sticker. It shows a Skinhead Jason from the Friday The 13th movies but he has braces and wallet chain with "SKINHEAD AND RUDE GIRLS SKALLOWEEN 2018".

Inside there are five people - the room has no chairs and the walls are crumbling in places, through the club darkness I can see cartoon skulls in the mural and layers of posters. I'm not sure if this is a legit club or squat. The DJ has on a tight, pale blue, lonsdale polo shirt, thin braces and rolled jeans. He has a full mop of hair though, and thick glasses and a beard with no moustache. He's playing mostly reggae but slowly mixing in northern soul, the only guy dancing is a young-looking lad dressed in black coat black shoes black hat, all that's missing is the Cadillac and I'd say the boy's a timebomb. He's dancing hard and when I see him later with his sunglasses off his eyes are almost all pupils. I get a drink from the bar, such as it is, and settle against the wall, watching the room as it begins to fill.

I'd guess there're around forty people here now, although it is hard to tell because nearly everyone is dancing. A few people are in fancy dress, I've spotted a V for Vendetta guy and The Demon: not "a" demon but a man in silver platforms, a silver jumpsuit, topped off with black curly hair and face painted to a near perfect Gene Simmons replica, so white it seems to glow.

Dominating the dance floor are a couple in their forties - full skinheads, the girl's hair only a fringe and two sideburns. The guy, mutton chops only. They're both white and look British. I would ask but I don't want to disturb them - they seem lost in the music but also at home together, spinning and curling, legs loose and shuffling, northern soul dancing in Central America.

The music changes to ska and the lights, the beer and the stabbing trumpets fill me with joy and silliness. Sometimes accidents can be happy, like finding here tonight. I'm watching Mexicans skank to songs my uncles would demand at weddings. Two white guys come in, they stand immobile in the middle of the floor as it erupts around them to a two tone version of the James Bond theme, they take in the crowd, and leave. But the crowd doesn't notice or care, it's one of those scenes I love; they're not here to judge or to be judged, they're here to be seen in the most modern sense of the word, noticed, acknowledged, validated as equals. They're here to share a thing they love and celebrate by giving themselves completely to it.

Some new wave punk is creeping into the set, the crowd bounce along. The lights catch the transparent, coloured vinyl 45s dangling from the stage. The beginning licks of Echo Beach slink out of the speakers. A song about longing, about a place you can never quite get too. Echo Beach isn't a real place but she longs to transcend her mundanity and get there anyway. The shyness and embarrassment melt away and I lose myself into the crowd dancing and laughing, swallowed and digested into the lights and music and a new family of letting go.

****

I'm trapped in a supermarket. My head is thumping and my legs are weak from dancing last night. I only wandered in here out of curiosity and almost immediately got chased down by a security guard who insisted on putting a sticker on my bottle of Dr Pepper which I think is some sort of anti-theft measure. From what I can tell, a Mexican supermarket is almost the same as an English supermarket, except a Mexican supermarket has no pretence at what it is - a huge room with food in it. There're no false ceilings, no fluorescent lighting chasing the shadows from every corner, no thought about 'user narrative' - just seven brands of noodles and an aisle for bread. I'm not trapped because I can't find the exit - I can see the exits - it's just to get to them you have to walk through the checkouts which are narrow perspex corridors which bring to mind something you'd see at a high grade abattoir. I'm already at the point of the hangover where I have the guilt sweats as it is. I'm not prepared to squeeze down the payment tubes and explain why I haven't bought anything in a language I don't speak. I have to buy something, but what? It has to be something non-suspicious. I construct a whole backstory of running out of deodorant but having very specific allergies so needing to come to the supermarket rather than the twenty other places I could have gone on the way. I spend way too long deliberately reading the ingredients of various deodorants to sell the bit before going to check out.

I'm walking out of the supermarket when I see him, peeking out from a poster board covered in flyers. Mr

Death is right there, on the top corner of a wrestling poster. I shift some of the paper covering it, in the middle is a ring and around it are various lucha wrestlers in masks trying to express how badass they are through various shoulder clenches and staring. The one at the top has a black mask with white vinyl shaping a skull. His eyes are soft hazelnut and relaxed, if distant, which is far more intimidating that the covered snarls the other wrestlers seem to be affecting under their masks. Intimidating, but welcoming. It's him, Mr Death. I clear out before my deodorant cover is blown.

****

I've found the hostel where the tour is meeting but I don't have any cash on me, luckily I'm 45 minutes early so I'm walking the nearby blocks in an ever increasing spiral pattern looking for an ATM. Sunset isn't for another couple of hours but it's dark out. Heavy clouds fill the sky and the promise of rain makes the frustration of not being able to find a cash machine so much worse. I've probably mentioned the shops in Mexico tend to be in districts, well around here it's the music district. This block has keyboards hanging in every window like pig flanks in a butchers, the next one brass instruments, I'm supposed to be meeting my tour in 20 minutes and I can buy a trumpet more easily than I can find a bank machine.

As I walk out of the bank's ATM antechamber the rain finally comes down in hefty splats, disconcertingly warm and slow, like they're being thrown by a bored god.

I'm not dressed for it, no one is. No one is running for shelter or reaching for umbrellas. I'm jogging to get to my tour and the rain is mostly missing me.

Now the rain sounds heavy from inside the van. There are 15 of us: an old American couple, a group of Koreans who may or may not be a family, two men in their thirties who sound Russian but haven't exchanged a word to each other since we left the hostel bar. Only three of us are wearing the wrestling masks we were handed as we got on the bus. Me, the Canadian guy next to me who is also called Dan and a lovely Welsh girl called Mia who can't stop giggling. The rain is drowning out the tour guide whose Spanish is hard to follow anyway. Me, Dan and Mia are taking it in turns to pose as if we're deeply interested in what he's saying despite the masks.

"But before we go we do SHOTS!" We all hear that. The tour guide cracks open a bottle and pours then distributes plastic thimbles of tequila, including the driver.

"Cheers!"

"Iechyd da!"

"Geonbae!"

"За встречу!"

And we pull off. As soon as the tour guide sits down Mia leans over to me and New Dan.

"Take this," she hands over her tequila.

"You don't want it?" I ask.

"Oh I haven't been able to drink tequila since I was 19," she says. I gesture to New Dan, he shakes his head.

"That's all you buddy," I knock it back before I think about it. The trick with shots, like a lot of things I've figured, is to do it without dwelling on it. Worrying about something is suffering twice as someone once said. While I'm doing that I can see the Russian guys handing their shots back.

"Well take them," says Mia, as he does so the Korean family starts to pass theirs back too. Now Mia, me and New Dan have two more shots each.

"I'm not doing eight shots," I say.

"There are only six," New Dan points out.

"I've already done two?" I say.

"Well I'll be sick," says Mia as seriously as she can through her wrestling mask.

"Okay, I'll do another one," says New Dan.

"Good work," I say and quickly throw back the rest before common sense catches up with me.

The traffic is heavy tonight and through the breath-smeared windows I can see the rain turns Mexico City noir; figures silhouetted against graffiti scratched windows, dramatic slashes of light from doors left ajar offering warm forbidden glimpses, abandoned buildings backlit from the strobes of passing police cars.

We've been in the same spot for a while now and the tour guide is looking back at us then out of the window, even leaning out at one point. He makes a decision.

Lucha Wrestling is massive in Mexico. There are two arenas in Mexico City both holding weekly matches and bigger monthly events that pull in thousands of spectators.

"We'll get off the bus here - stay together." We jump off and follow him through the traffic jam towards a municipal building, there's a mass of people in various queues, or just milling about. Our guide takes us just past the crowd to a separate break in the cord barriers. A big guy stops me and points to my wallet chain, apparently it is not allowed, I don't have the time, language, or sobriety to argue. My tour guide is just ahead about to be swallowed by the increasingly frenetic crowd. I quickly detach it, hand it to the guy and catch up.

New Dan has saved me a seat - we're midway up the seating. In the middle of the arena is a wrestling ring, from that is a metal walkway leading to a set with entrance curtains, a huge screen and balconies. There are two rows of young women wearing slightly less than cheerleaders, doing simple choreography in a holding pattern while the crowd is seated. The music intensifies and a man enters. He announces something and an impossible number of wrestlers swarm the ring and immediately start attacking each other. The damp crowd erupts, shouting and pointing while wrestlers take it in turns to slap, pound, and push each other. The effect as a whole is an overwhelming circus of violence until you focus individually and see the repeated patterns and theatrical overreactions. Most of the wrestlers are masked, no sign of Mr Death yet though.

If you squint, it looks like a gay porn parody of the Mighty Morphin Power Rangers. The action has focused somewhat, with six or so wrestlers sharing the ring. The rest outside, while active, are careful not to pull focus. Inside the ring the wrestlers are throwing moves and counter moves, all while avoiding each other and staying in their identifiable characters. The Faces cheer the crowd and help each other, while The Heels gouge and sneer.

The crowd are still on their feet and I can't help but notice they're having a much better time than, say, New Dan, who is sitting there with a look of bemused enjoyment. I decide to get invested; I order a drink from the guy selling crisps covered in hot sauce and decide to pick a wrestler from each match. The first wrestler I pick has a red cross across his silver mask and a chiseled but agile, tan body. I dub him 'La Cruz'. He seems to be doing well, he's grappling with a meatier guy in a green mask and trunks and is winning until another already disqualified wrestler reaches into the ring and pulls La Cruz's feet from under him. BANG, he hits the deck.

"TWAT!" I shout at the Heel jeering the crowd as he runs away up the ramp. New Dan jerks at my sudden shout, which settles into our new dynamic, me shouting at the wrestling while he squirms in confused embarrassment. It's down to my guy and Green Mask. La Cruz is trapped in the corner while Green Mask is punching down on his head, he's paused while La Cruz is dazed and takes a run up to body slam him. Gaining momentum, Green Mask is bouncing from rope to rope and finally launches himself at La Cruz, but La Cruz catches Green Mask mid-air. He roars at the crowd and

we roar back as he swings Green Mask over the top
rope. He wins. Mentally, so do I. I order another drink.

My voice feels scratchy and tight. The last match is a
three-on-three bout. The obvious bad guys come to
the ring, none of them are wearing masks but two are
wearing suits and they are accompanied by a heavy
Japanese guy dressed like Fred Flintstone with a bone
in his hair. The camera pulls close to his face and a
thick trail of drool dangles out of his mouth. The good
guys all wear masks including one who the crowd love.
Personally, I can't tell the difference between the three
although the crowd's favourite seems to be more oiled
than the rest of them. I'm cheering for the Suits and
their pet caveman.

The Main Suit is against Greasy Hero and losing.
Greasy Hero is keeping him in the middle of the ring
so he can't tag out, and Greasy Hero is spinning and
flipping Main Suit senseless. Up until now I've forgotten
my mission: no wrestler in a skull mask has come out
and with all the drinks and shouting I've forgotten I'm
looking, but then, there he is. No fanfare or entrance
music, he's a big guy running down to the ring. Greasy
hero doesn't see him coming, Death Mask is behind
him with a chair. BAM! Greasy Hero is floored. Death
Mask calmly walks away. Main Suit is on the floor too
but is managing to crawl to his corner. He tags Japanese
Caveman who gets into the ring just as Greasy Hero
shakily stands up. Japanese Caveman is beyond fucking
about and, before the crowd can warn Greasy Hero,
Japanese Caveman walks up and kicks him squarely in
the balls. Greasy Hero's feet leave the floor. Bells ring,

bout over, but the ref and the others are chased away. The suits stand over Greasy Hero and peel his mask off.

It's still raining hard when we get outside. The gutters are deep and fast moving and the crowd seems more panicked as the surges from behind push, edging us outside. The tour guide does not stop for a head count, he glances at us and sprints for the van. We follow, weaving between the still and honking traffic. We're soaked by the time we get in the van, and me and Mia have put our masks back on.

"Enjoy that?" says New Dan. There's a gentle mocking I can hear in his tone, but the fact is I did, way more than he did.

"So much fun," I croak back.

The bar is just closing as I get back. There's one guy at one of the tables at the back talking into a tech slab that lights his animated face. He's wearing a shirt and tie, but also board shorts and flip flops. The only other light is from the altar which now has a few more candles and flowers. I squelch on over. The sign has been changed: "Dias De los Ahogados - today we remember victims of drowning or the sea". Water is dripping off me and pooling on the marble floor. I take a peek under the plaster in my psyche, remembering being in that sea. My heart lurches a little, but is not too sore and I can stop thinking about it if I want. There's an unlit candle and a box of matches so I light one and say something, not for me, but for everyone who wasn't as lucky. Suddenly,

I don't want to be in these wet, clinging, clothes so I swamp off to bed.

****

The metro this morning isn't as full, but I'm distracted by the lack of familiar weight of my wallet chain against my thigh. Partly, because I'm trying to be more alert to pickpockets and partly because, if I let my attention wander I get the heart sink moment of 'SHIT you forgot something'. I've worn a wallet chain since I was a teenager. I think I lost three wallets in the space of a month and decided it's very unlikely my debauched lifestyle was going to change, so I was going to have to resort to more practical measures. Sure, over the years I've had some hassle getting into venues, and I've missed more than one train or bus because the chain has snaked into the gaps of the bench I'm sitting on and got stuck, but it's familiar heft is now as part of me as my grey-blue eyes or changeable stubbornness. This morning, the sign next to the altar was for Los Olvidados' - the forgotten. Perhaps fitting that I'm heading to the market known as El Chopo, the 'youth culture' market - this 'youth culture' being mostly, in this case, rock and alternative culture. Named after a building at the university where it was originally sited, El Chopo in some form has been around since the early sixties where it started as a meeting place for the emerging hippie culture. After a ban on touring rock bands which started in the early seventies became a de facto ban on rock music in general, driving it underground, the market became an important hub not only for alternative culture, but alternative and revolutionary thinking.

End of the Line. I follow the crowd out of the station and look for signs to the market. If I squint my eyes and look at the crowd, I can see there's a higher density of black T-shirts heading down the road. A little further down, there is someone in full punk regalia: spiked hair, studded leather jacket, and tartan bondage trousers. He's sitting with a sneer behind a laid-out T-shirt on which has been spread a small selection of bootlegged CDs with photocopied covers. Walking past, I hope that wasn't it. But I needn't have worried; between two rows of buildings, a road, no more than an alley really, is slowly alive with activity. Metal beams being slotted together, tarpaulin being stretched, and crusties, punks and traders gently folding clothes and aesthetically adjusting their displays just so. It seems I'm early. The internet tells me this is a high crime area but that's at odds with how it feels on a lazy morning. The sun is shining and the buildings either side of the main road are painted with colourful murals. Somewhere, a blues band is practicing and the music blends with the traffic and backyard conversations. It's hard to believe crime happens here. I'll still feel better when I get a chain for my wallet, though.

"Torta de chorizo?" The lady at the cafe doesn't wait for me to answer and places the sandwich in front of me anyway.

"Muchas gracias," I say to no one in particular as she's already left to man the smoothie counter window, serving passing customers in the street. A green, ex-military van pulls up on the street, uncomfortably close to the cafe's door. A man jumps out, black vest, combat trousers and boots. He's got a black bandanna with a skull pattern around his wrist and a thick chain from his belt loop to his pocket. From the back of the van he's shifting large bags of fruit into the cafe, making chat with the waitresses. One of them must have mentioned me, their only customer, because he non-so-subtly looks over. We make eye-contact and he smiles, giving me a firm up-nod of recognition.

Alternative rock culture the world over has a habit of hoovering up all the misfits and weirdos, giving you a family of sorts. I'm from the generation that saw the tribalism of different youth cultures erode and all but disappear; rap merged with metal, The Prodigy got heavy enough to be played in even the darkest metal clubs and, for ten years or so, everything was a remix or mash-up with layers of pastiche and irony so thick no one could really cling to the divisions as stridently as they could before. The next real alternative tribe to emerge after that wasn't so lucky. Emo was earnest - devoid of the irony and remove that runs through gen x like fat marbling a fine steak. Emos were mocked for their tight trousers, back combed hair with fringes, performative self-harm, and the mainstream pop edge a lot of their music had. In the same way older punks scoffed at the next wave of supposed 'pop' punk, the alternative community looked down on emo.

I'm thinking about emo because those criticisms were much harsher in Mexico and culminated ten years ago in a wave of attacks against emo kids at the El Chopo markets. It started when a VJ/personality went on a tirade against the emo subculture, describing it as a 'stupid, weak movement' with 'no ideas or music'. I suppose in the less tolerant macho culture of Mexico a subculture based on emotionality and with some femme aspects to the aesthetic was always going to be viewed with mistrust. For a while emo kids were attacked on sight. I never liked emo, partly because the music, with some exceptions, was generally bad and, if I'm honest, it happened after me - it wasn't mine in the same way as say nu-metal or thrash. Emos have mostly aged out now, the refugees absorbed back into the rock scene in general. Death comes to us all, even scenes, ideas and movements.

The market shows no signs of such divisions, the tight jeans of the emo being sold next to the leather chaps of the biker and the striped tartan of the punk. I find a heavy wallet chain on a stand next to a stall selling T-shirts with designs from cult movies. Towards the back of the market the stalls thin out, a stage is set at the back with a low roof of tarpaulin. In the background there are the giant white struts of an electricity substation spilling out with a complex net of wires and tubes. The crowd of thirty or so people in front of the stage look black and homogeneous compared to the defined but complex lines that take up most of the available sky. A metal band thrash through their set while the edges of the crowd melt off to the food trucks opposite. Attached to the market, but not quite part of it, are the older gentlemen, mostly in hobo denim and wild beards, sat with their record collections and bootleg tapes spread on blankets. They browse each other's wares without venturing into the market proper.

On my way back through it's comforting to be surrounded by familiar brands, images and logos. The rock world has its pantheon of new and old gods, and the grammar of its worship translates across the world. I see Death everywhere, his grinning face on shirts, belt buckles, rings, hats, cloaks, bags. He's on posters and pointing from tattoos. He's everywhere, but not really. Just an image, a taboo broken and rebroken. As western culture becomes more sanitised and euphemistic towards death the alternative subculture becomes more embracing of it. From the theatrical memento mori of the goths, to the performative nihilism of grunge, death is a weapon that has been used to shock, offend, and ward off the complacency of normality and the thin veneer of the mainstream. If I am to find Death I need to leave this fun house hall of mirrors and try elsewhere.

****

There's a special type of headache I get just before a thunderstorm, a pressure that leans on my frontal cortex and cleverly disconnects the part of my memory that realises the headache is weather related at all and lets me worry about tumours or brain parasites until the rain finally breaks and I remember in a wash of relief. Thank the gods the endorphins from the tattoo I got this morning are working their magic, not only on the stinging forearm but also the crushing effect of the heavy, near-black sky that has turned Mexico City into twilight all day. I'm back at the rooftop bar in the first hostel and from here I can see the edges of the cloud and the blue sky underneath, just like the edges of the headache are expanding in my head. Strictly speaking, I shouldn't be here as I'm not a resident but the door code hasn't been changed since I was last here and none of the staff bother to check your wristband if you're white enough.

Today, according to the altar at the hostel, is the day we honour our ancestors and those we have lost in the last year. I've been thinking all day of what I've lost this year. The literal love of my life cheated on me; not just physically, but emotionally, falling in love with someone else. The darkness in my headache makes it easier to confront the darkness I think I've been dwelling on since all this started, would Her dying be less painful? Is this whole quest a distraction from a more painful truth? I'm nauseous and take a swig of Corona in order to taste something other than my churning stomach acid. My head is at the bottom of a ocean. I can taste salt. My head is in my hands, finger pressing into my skin. What hurts? The headache or the knowledge she's actually better off without you?

There's a flash, and a bang like the building is split in two. Then one dot of rain hits the table, then another. Soon, waves of rain bounce from every surface. My head is clearer, blessed. The rain stings my eyes, I'd been crying. Another flash and a bang of thunder rolling around and I'm laughing, running for cover. I once had a tarot deck for nearly twenty years; I loved the cards' style, both heavily abstracted and luridly real. The Death card had a sky almost the same as this one. Underneath that sky wasn't the biblical pale rider in black plate of the traditional deck but a pale man drawing back a veil. Death in the Tarot stands for change. Dying is change at its most brutal, but things must die for new things to live. I've lost a lot this last year, not only Her, but my life with Her, who I was when I was with Her, and my future, a future I could imagine for the first time in my life. What can grow in the wake of all that?

My tattoo itches. Looking down through the clingfilm I can see the circle with the snake head, a snake eating its own tail. The ouroboros, a symbol used by alchemists to depict the endless cycle of life and death, a visual riddle that clears my mind in the same way zen koans did when I was a teenager. For me, now a permanent reminder implicit in every beginning is an end, but in that end, a beginning. Or at least the space for a beginning.

"Why did you change your mind?" says the tattooist, while he waits for the template to print "Do you still want to see the Santa Muerte one?"

"Santa Muerte?" I ask.

"In Mexico we call this image 'Santa Muerte'." He refers to a picture I originally sent him of the Grim Reaper "In Espanol, death is 'las' which is lady, she has become like a saint."

"Saint death?" I ask.

"Si, people say she is saint for drug dealers or whatever, but she is saint that helps everyone, does not discriminate."

Another flash and the roll of thunder is later this time, I feel fresh, new, clear.

Finding it by accident was easy, but now that I'm looking for it, the little St Christopher shrine is proving more elusive. Eventually, I recognise the wall and follow it down until the rocks start to get looser and eventually crumble. And there it is. I'm not big into prayer but I . replaced the flowers with some nice blue ones I swiped out of a garden on the way and lit a candle in a jar that was on one of the tables at a restaurant near the hotel. The least I can do for a second chance.

10. The Death You Know, The Better

The receptionist is looking at me patiently. The new hostel I'm checking into is either overcharging me or - and it's becoming increasingly more likely the more I think about it - I really fucked up the decimal place when trying to convert the money back to pounds when I booked it. But it's Halloween, the day before a major festival in the country's capital. The chances of me finding anywhere else to stay are slim to none. I hand over all the money I have on me, she hands me a key and a token for a free beer.

The hostel is a self-styled gallery concept, which amounts to white walls with mid-range art and illustration prints. The only other person in the dorm is a thin bald guy in harem trousers, sitting cross legged on his bunk fiddling with a sound file on his laptop. I know he's French somehow, even before he introduces himself. His name is Christophe and he's writing some techno tracks. He plays me some.

"Nice," I say "sounds like some trance in there too."

"Yes, you are right." He sounds surprised.

"I used to go clubbing a lot, there was a huge techno scene where I'm from," I say.

"Oh, where?"

"You won't have heard of it, Birmingham," I say. "England," I add in case it's not clear.

"Oh Atomic Jam, and God's House?"

"Yes!" I say. "I used to go to every one for a couple of years, especially House Of God."

"Who did you see?" he asks.

"Surgeon, Ritchie Hawtin and Dave Clarke once."

"Phat Planet!" exclaims Christophe.

"Yes!" Christophe and me do the iconic drum line with our mouths for a bit, then a bit more.

"Well cool man, I'm going to go get that free drink from the bar" I say.

"Cool," says Christophe coolly and goes back to his laptop.

Downstairs, the bar is essentially just a corridor to the bathroom painted black, with a partition running the length of it. By the door is a fridge stacked with beer and I imagine, with some awkwardness, it's conceivable the bartender could reach it and get to the beer. A youngish man in his thirties who I noticed earlier in the back office of reception sticks his head in.

"The bar's open in five minutes, someone will be along soon," he gives me a customer service smile and disappears before I can say anything. Two lads bumble in. They're both the type of English lad I haven't seen in months, one is wearing a West Ham top, the other is in a Nike sweatshirt.

"I like your hair," says one of them in acknowledgement. I hear it a lot and, as such, have figured out there are three main ways that phrase is intended. One is genuine, some people I've discovered like the odd colours I turn my hair. Another way can be translated "you've just noticed me staring at your hair and now it'd be more awkward now not to acknowledge it" which is fine, sweet in a way. The third translates to "I don't like your hair, it confuses me and I don't like things I don't understand, you owe me an explanation." The lads climbing onto the stools next to me have definitely veered off two and into three territory, so they get the number three response.

"Thanks, it's natural actually."

"Naaahhhh," says the one in the West Ham top. Not sure if I'm joking. Nike sweatshirt has barely sat down before he says,

"I ain't waitin, see you upstairs, yeah?" with a not so subtle touch of his nostril and a sniff. West ham top nods and turns to me.

"English, right?"

"Yeah, Birmingham."

"Birminum yeah, I've been up a few times. Villa or Blues?"

"I don't really follow football," He deflates slightly at this "but I was dragged up a Blues fan, nearly shit myself when I saw the claret and blue but that's the hammers right?" I'm nearly exhausting my football bluff vocabulary.

"Too right," he says, relieved. "Mikey," he shakes my hand, "that was AJ but he's still spinning from last night?"

"Large one?" I ask.

"Yeah, that twat passes out in the club toilets, club closes. They kick us out with him still locked inside. And get this. They say they won't let him out without us paying them."

"No shit?"

"Straight up, I thought the bouncer was going to rob me when he walked me to the cashpoint."

"Wow, that's sketchy as fuck."

"Yeah, he was fucked up though, didn't know what was going on, they kept him in the minging bogs asking him for his passport."

"Shit."

"Shit's right mate, I can tell ya."

Mikey is affable, we chat and he asks me why I'm in Mexico and I tell him a short version about being just out of a relationship.

"No way man, me too, this was supposed to be our trip, then she goes and cheats on me. So I'm like fuck her, and I bring AJ instead." As he's talking, Christophe joins us and surprises me by taking a place behind the bar and starting to set up, he looks over at me and Mikey in a way that I can't quite understand.

"Beer?" says Christophe, specifically to me.

"Yes please," I say. Mikey, getting nothing of what Christophe is putting out says, "Let me get 'em in."

"Nah, it's cool" I say, "I've got a token for the first one." Christophe looks relieved.

"Just go in the fridge with anything from the top two shelves," he says.

"Get me one too Danny," says Mikey, I do. Christophe takes the token off me and the money off Mikey.

"And I'll get the next one," he says.

"I've got to say Mikey, I appreciate the offer but I can't do rounds, I've got no cash until I got to an ATM."

"Fak orrf," he laughs, "I'm buying you one." He holds his bottle up for a toast, "birds" he says. I chink bottles with him and as I'm taking a sip he says "fuck 'em". Which makes beer come out of my nose. Mikey laughs too. We chat and I try to include Christophe who remains aloof, different to how I found him upstairs. Mikey is checking his phone and I mouth.

"You okay?" over to Christophe, he nods towards Mikey and half shakes his head. Mikey probably rubbed him the wrong way with some misplaced banter I figure. We drink the last of our beers, Mikey jumps off his stool stands close to me and says, as subtle as I think he can.

"We got some sniff upstairs if you fancy a tootle, it's fucking gear." In my head, I'm thinking 'fuck it why not' but I make eye contact with Christophe over his shoulder. Christophe widens his eyes and shakes his head 'no'.

"You know what Mikey, I'm going to say no, tempted and all that, but I'm not a big coke guy."

"Suits yourself," he goes to go but leans back, "if you want a blast later give us a shout". He slaps my back as he passes. Once he's gone, Christophe comes over.

"You okay mate?"

"Yes," he says flatly, and opens another beer and puts it in front of me.

"Christophe, I've got no cash mate" he gives me the free beer token.

"No problem," he says distractedly, he looks at me "stay here with me".

"Sure," I say and take a swig while he carries on cutting lemons. I've finished the beer when Christophe becomes distracted by what's going on in reception. I look around to see AJ and Mikey barrelling out the door with their suitcases.

"Isn't…"

"In a minute," interrupts Christophe, then "they are gone."

"What was that about?" I ask. Christophe looks looser, more relaxed now.

"Management was waiting to catch them doing coke… if you had gone up with him you would have been thrown out too." I let how close it just had been sink in.

"Wow thanks," I say. Christophe shrugs but with a smile. "Is it that strict here then?"

"Not really, but those two are not discreet. They were telling everyone about their cocaine they bought up from Columbia."

They took it across the border?"

"Yes, very bad."

"Why didn't they kick off?" I ask, thinking about every coked-up cockney I'd ever met being told something they didn't like. "Cause a fuss," I clarify when Christophe looks confused.

"The manager told me he was going to tell them he has called the police."

"Shit, they'll get arrested?" I say

"Oh no, he won't call them, that'd be bad for everyone."

"Well I owe you man, fancy going out tonight? Go celebrate Halloween?"

"Oh non, I'm working. After, I might go upstairs and smoke some weed, say hello when you get in." I remember the times I've done drugs while being abroad, the occasional social toke, that one time I was spiked at Mardi Gras and that time I was nearly drugged in Australia

****

Blinking, we step out of the bar into the unforgiving Australian sunlight. I fumble for my shades. Aussie Dan doesn't react, not even to squint. His face is a permanent squint, like he's always angrily trying to understand the world. Aussie Dan is a bear of a man, a builder by trade. Aussie Dan isn't called Aussie Dan as a way to differentiate himself from me, by rights, I should be English Dan. Aussie Dan is so called because even other Australians find him very Australian.

"Right, that was good for starters." Aussie Dan has taken it as a point of national pride that he must drink me under the table, hence drinking for the last three hours in a hole bar in a dirty corner of Kings Cross.

"Getting close to closing time mate," he says. At this point in Australia the bars closed for a few hours in the afternoon to

encourage people to go home and eat something instead of going straight to the pub after work and staying there. Or at least this is how Aussie Dan explained it to me.

"No worries, though mate, I'll find a place," he adds. Yes, he really does say "no worries" and, after a few weeks in Australia, so will you, a lot. Aussie Dan winks at me and slaps me on the shoulder putting it back into place after he dislocated it earlier doing the same thing when I beat him at pool.

Aussie Dan sets off further into Kings Cross. At this time Kings Cross was the less polished part of Sydney: bars, houses of ill repute and backpacker hostels. When I arrived in Sydney, I told the taxi driver at the airport to "take me where the action is." He took me straight here and I haven't left yet.

By the time I catch up with Aussie Dan he's arguing with a man in the booth at the top of some stairs. I can't see the signage.

"Twenty bucks each," says the man behind the counter, surprised that haggling is now part of his, until now, relatively simple job.

"Here's 10 for us both." Aussie Dan hands the man some money. "Danny, in here." As I follow him the woman outside handing out flyers says "Live Sex - all real, all good."

Downstairs is gloomy, but it's not not just the lighting - there is a cloud of shame. The black walls are clammy. There's a couple of men at a table right next to the stage. A waitress in a bikini meets and seats us. She isn't surly, but she's not friendly either. Something's off. She hands us a laminated menu with only two items on it; beer is eight dollars and cocktails are four dollars. The waitress doesn't leave us so we can pretend to deliberate about what we'll have.

"Two cocktails please," I say.

"I'll have two cocktails too please," says Aussie Dan. The waitress pauses.

"You can only have them one at a time… they are strong" she says.

"That's fine," I reply. As we're ordering, a group of four or so men are led downstairs by the woman outside. They're seated behind us.

"Cocktails all round lads?" she asks. They all cheer.

The waitress returns with our drinks. They're red, like thick cranberry juice. Aussie dan is so Australian he takes a sip after removing the straw. Aussie men don't use straws. I take a sip.

"Dan?" I say, hesitantly. He turns around and takes another sip. I put my hand out over his glass. "Mate - have you ever done drugs?"

"Not me mate, mug's game."

"Well I have, lots of them."

"Yeah?"

"Yeah, and this drink tastes of drugs." I take another sip, it's gritty with a bitter aftertaste that is almost hidden by the sweetness and sharpness of the cranberry.

"You sure?" says Aussie Dan.

"Fairly mate, can't you taste it?"

"Fucking no."

"Well I'm not drinking mine" I say.

"I thought you liked drugs."

"Sometimes, but I don't like mystery drugs in a murder basement," I hiss. Behind us, the group of lads are necking their cocktails. Aussie Dan calls the waitress over.

"We're not drinking these," he hands her our drinks.

"Why not" she says evenly.

"Tastes like someone fucked with them - we'll have a beer instead." Wordlessly, she takes our cocktails away and reappears with bottles of VB. She goes to leave but Aussie Dan holds up his hand for her to wait and watches as I take a cautious swig of each of the stubbies, I give Aussie Dan the nod and he dismisses the waitress.

The live sex show is a disappointment and under threat from trading standards depending on how broad your definition of sex is. For me, watching a waitress strip and wank off a member of the audience isn't really included. I don't know who to feel sorrier for as the poor guy is laid on a towel and, after a few minutes fruitless fellatio, she mounts him and pretends he's not soft. Me and Dan watch from the corners of our eyes out of embarrassment for all involved.

The lads behind us, now on their second or third cocktail have been joined by ladies, some in underwear, some in bikinis. The ladies are flirting and sitting on the lads laps. I notice all of them are drinking beer not cocktails. One by one these lads follow the ladies through a door by the bar.

"Let's get the fuck out of here," I say to Aussie Dan.

"Fucking truth," he says.

****

It's the 31st of October and it might be because it's Wednesday, or that the American Halloween virus hasn't not spread everywhere yet, or that most of the parties happened on Saturday, but the streets are emptier than normal. This new hostel is five minutes away from the Zona Rosa and my feet pull me that way.

Before I checked out of the Art Deco hostel this morning I lit a candle at the altar; today is the day we remember souls in limbo. The club I'm in is open-plan and dirty, The condensation tracing lines through the dust on the walls. The toilets have saloon doors, I imagine to ensure single occupancy. Someone has been sick in the urinal and now it's a brimming piss pond. I sit near the back of the tiny main room people-watching. There're a few people in fancy dress, but only one has totally gone for it; an angel wearing silver short shorts, silver body glitter and nothing else, is breaking every-body's heart on the dancefloor. His flesh shimmers as he swirls and bounces, eyes closed in love with the music, with moving, with the moment as it happens.

The church has no official stance on limbo - the corporeal state, not the dance - although the big See hasn't mentioned much about either. Limbo is not referenced directly in the bible just inferred by the gaps in the heavenly protocol. It's an edge place: the edge of heaven or hell, or both depending who you listen too. Those in limbo aren't lost, just waiting at the edges, making the most of it, I hope.

The dance floor is fuller now, but I'm happier here at the back with the lights and the wash of bass rattling my chest. Watching who's making out with who, who's dancing to try and hook up and who's just dancing. The friends, the thought-we-were-friends, the thought-we-were-just-friends. The topless, the bottomless tops, the hopeless. All of us saved by the music, the lights, our connection of one moment, the moment we're in, here, at the edge.

****

It wasn't dark when we set off but we hit traffic two hours ago and we're still slowly making our way out of the city. The highway east of Mexico City rises out of the nesting sprawl like the legs of a sleeping spider, and as the roads turn south you can see the scope of the city, endless lights and stories, buildings and ruins. Inside the bus other backpackers are playing a drinking game with a bottle of Mezcal, it's something complicated with numbers and hand gestures. I've got to focus - tonight must be the night that I find him. Tonight is the first proper night of Día de los Muertos. Having no luck in the city so far, I booked this excursion to San Andres Mixquic, a traditional small town. We drive through a town and the streets are busy with young children wearing masks or sometimes full costumes. They're running from shop to shop, all of them open and brightly lit, the kids carrying buckets of sweets. Most are accompanied or at least followed by a smiling but exasperated adult.

We park on a dirt road next to a row of garages. The tour guide tells us, "It's about a mile to the village, we will have to walk from here, please keep up. If we get separated, meet back here at eleven." I look around for a landmark, there's nothing but garages and five identical buses.

We follow the tour guide and dive right into a market, but it's a festival market. As well as the usual fare of knock off fashion, handmade souvenirs and jewellery there are carnival games, dart stalls, coconuts shies, flashing toys, stuffed toys, poseable toys. Giant teddy bears hang like the grapes of tantalus. The speakers, whoops, and jingles drown out the sound of the crowd except for the odd shrill of laughter. And the smell of food grabs me by the guts and reminds me of how hungry I am. Fresh fried churros, salty butter dripping off glistening corn, the sizzle and smoke of grilling meat.

Getting through the crowd is slow work, every so often the tour guide's cap stops, steps to the side and bobs up and down as he tries to count the group together. It's frustrating; not only am I craving food but I'm hungry to see what's next. The fiesta stalls are not meant to be deliberated over, they urge you to go through in a blur of colours and sensations.

We stop again right next to a grill selling metre-long sticks wrapped in glazed meat, the sound of which is an incredible hissing. Last time we stopped was for nearly ten minutes while somebody caught up after browsing phone cases so I make a decision. I go to the stall and order. The meat is delicious, tender with a charred crust and a fruity BBQ glaze. When I look up from my steak sabre for the cap of the tour guide, it's not there. They've moved on without me. If I boot on now I can probably catch them up but pushing through the crowd with a food baton will be difficult and I'm not throwing it away. It's perhaps lucky that I have been unknowingly training for this moment my entire life. I don't know what the record is for speed eating over a metre of freshly cooked meat, but I'd still put money I beat the record. My orgy of carnivorism only stopping when I find myself sucking the stick for its absorbed juices.

I'm moving through the crowd more gracefully than I have any right to, seeing the amount of food I've just eaten. I'm focusing on the crowd a couple of metres ahead of me so I can see which way to step next, but also trying to keep aware so I can spot the tour guide ahead and trying my best not to get distracted by the pretty flashing lights. But ahead, just rounding the corner, a sweep of cloak, the glimpse of porcelain bone. Probably nothing, keep going. But again, it's him, Mr Death, round that corner. I don't know what to do, leave the safety of the tour group and go chasing a figure? Or push forward to the tour where I am supposed to be? Where do I belong?

I've chased Mr Death over an ocean and a couple of continents, and frankly I'm sick of it. If I find the answers to the questions, then great. But running after ghosts is no way to live. I'm missing life to find Death to ask him why we don't get as much life as we think we should have. And if the tour guide doesn't want to wait for me, fine, I really don't need them. I choose neither. I choose to walk through the carnival and appreciate the moment I'm in. Not wrestling with unanswerable questions or forcing myself to be where I think I should. I laugh. Slowly browsing the beckoning lights and colours and games. I've been chasing shadows and there's a relief that comes with realising you can't catch a shadow, but its nothing compared to the feeling of turning around and feeling the light on my face for the first time since you started.

Out of the market now, but the crowd is thick like porridge, a lot of white faces like mine with cameras, some painted faces and masks too. A crowd thick enough to make doing anything but going in the same direction as everyone else difficult. Luckily everybody seems to be filtering into the monastery courtyard. I join a group of people by a large stone statue, its details lost in the dark, lit only by candle and the occasional phone flash. Another tour comes to the figure, their tour guide tells us this is Mictlanteuctli, his name literally means 'Lord of Mictlan', Mitctlan being the underworld. He was worshipped in this area before colonial rule, before the monastery was even built. The settlers outlawed it. His main festival was this time of year and possibly one of the roots of The Día de los Muertos. Mictlanteuctli worship involves sacrifice and even cannibalism, the tour guide relishes the last fact as if he were telling a story around a campfire and I become very conscious of my belly full of barely chewed meat. The group stops at one of the raised plant beds. It takes a while for everybody else to realise, but I can see them instantly. It's a pile of bones, broken, but clean. Two thigh bones, dust dry and black pitted with age, lay in a cross over the top of them. They're probably the remains of the monseniors and other important clergy found when the monastery was deconsecrated. I look around for Mr Death, but the crowd is moving and so am I.

I split from that group, they're taking a look at different altars called 'ofrendas'. I find myself in the churchyard.

The church is closed, but the grounds are open. There are hundreds of stone graves, and the umber glow of a thousand candles and orange marigolds make it seem warm, inviting even. Some people are walking around taking photos, a few others are just being, trying to take it all in. In the middle there's a large tiered altar in black stone, from behind its haloed in bright candlelight. I come off the path to investigate but soon realise there is no path between graves, no room at all in fact. I'm careful to place my feet only on the border bricks of the graves, mentally apologising as I go. The other people I've seen walking around must be nimble as hell, casually sacrilegious, or spirits themselves.

The altar is six foot and finished at the top with a plain stone cross. Between the rudimentary stone skulls carved into each shelf have been placed the yellow orange marigolds. Tall candles in holders flank each tier and on the first three tiers are piles of bones, some bright bleached white, some yellow, and some black with age. It looks like somebody had started to sort them into similar piles on the lowest tier, but the rest are just heaped and dotted with petals. In its own way, it's beautiful and I take a photo before playing blasphemy twister back to the path.

The main square is now full with what looks to be the entire village and its visitors. They're watching an older guy on stage, the song is finishing with a repeated refrain and everyone is singing with him. He holds the last note, breaks it to make a cheeky remark and the crowd collapses with laughter. He continues the note and finishes to a wave of applause and cheering, expertly letting it wash over him a little before talking again. My Spanish still hasn't gotten good enough to understand but the rhythms of his speech are warm and funny, this warmth is then reflected back from the crowd with wide-eyed affection. A few people in the crowd are drinking beer. The main stalls of the market don't sell it, neither do the few shops that have managed to stay open. I spot a couple of beer drinkers going down a side street, so I follow them. I'm greeted by a 7ft sculpture of a skeleton in a dress with a tiny baby skeleton in a sling on her back. A few yards further down two skeleton firefighters wrestle with a hose. The street is residential, lit by lanterns and fairy lights, every few yards is a thin skeleton sculpture or flower mosaic in orange and black. Some of the houses have opened their front rooms into makeshift cafes and some have small counters by their front door selling drinks and sweet breads. At one of these I buy a coke.

"Don't suppose you have beer at all - cerveza?" I ask the strong looking woman serving me.

"No allowed cerveza past eight," she says.

"I like the skeletons - las calaca," I say as I hand her the money.

"Si, we do them every year, money in the bucket for the village." She waves my change near one of the donation buckets, I nod and, pleased, she tosses it in.

"What are the little horses?" I nod at one of the stuffed horses I've spotted about "I saw them on the offerndos in the village."

"Today is for the little ones, la perro are guides, helps them on the other side."

"Perro is horse?" I ask.

"Dog," she says. "Dogs are guides for la alma, the soul".

I find the bus, mainly because I recognise our guide who
lost everyone so came back to the bus to wait. I found
him and the bus driver smoking. They assure me I'm not
late and, even if I wasn't, I'm not the last to arrive. Over
the street a crowd of very drunk tourists climb aboard
a bus nearly identical to our own. They're all in various
states of Woooo, a few with skull face paint blurred
around the mouth. There waving light up lightsaber toys
from the market. As I walk past the driver to get on the
bus he nods over to them, sighs, and tells the guide.

"Were losing our traditions."

****

Next day, back in Mexico City. Another market, another
yard of meat. This time I'm in the historic centre of
Coyoacán, a colonial square which is a focus of tourism;
an integral part of the local district economy. The
square is dominated by a stage with a dance troupe
fumbling through a routine, and a tent showing the
Disney film Coco - which based around The Day Of
The Dead - on a large screen. The crowd is mostly
families and there's lots of fancy dress, only a small
proportion of which seems to be Halloween or even
traditionally Mexican. I'm as out of place as I've ever
been; unseen, gliding through the realness of other
people's lives with my ghost passport.

Slipping down a side street away from the lights I hear some loud alley cat rockabilly, and a little further I see the lights of a bar; Bizarro Cafe. I have to go. Inside, it's a cross between a cowboy saloon and an industrial goth workshop; the tables are full but there's a seat at the bar. I ask for a beer and I'm given a litre in a solid glass tankard. The glass is cold to the touch. The solid front door is open and an evening around another market has left me with the first real chill since last winter. As I pick up the beer I catch the deep grey eyes of the guy in the stool next to me.

"Your health," I say before I drink.

"Up yours," he says, saluting me right back. I nearly choke on my beer. "You're English, right? You say 'up yours'?" he asks.

"Who taught you that?"

"My brother's wife, she is from Leeds, you know Leeds?, she taught me," he smiles. "Is it a joke?" he asks. I shake my head.

"No, I just wasn't expecting it," I stick out my hand "Danny".

"Cale," he says and shakes mine. Cale has shoulder length white hair and is wearing double denim, the jacket being nearer white than blue with patches that look older than me.

"How did you know I was English?" I ask.

"You speak like her."

"Is that where you learnt English? You speak it well."

"My mother was a Jew, she was from all over," he says.

"Doesn't that make you Jewish too?" Cale laughs, a lot.

"Maybe" he says eventually, "have you come to Mexico for the festival?"

"In a way," I hedge, "I'm here to find Death, la calaca." He takes this well, thinks for a moment.

"...and?" he prompts.

"Well, no luck so far."

"Good," he says flatly.

"Good?"

"Yes, it's not wise to attract Death's attention, I'm thinking" he says.

"Oh, I'm not wise," I say, taking another pull of beer, "know anything about the old gods?"

"I don't know if you noticed the churches, but this country is Catholic now," he smiles.

"Those churches are built using the stone of the old temples," I say.

"This is true."

"I was at the Museum of Anthropology today," I explain.

"Never been, is good?"

"You should, massive place."

"Massive?" he asks.

"Big," I say, "anyway, there's this god of the underground, big scary god, with a skull for a head. I can't pronounce his name, but it translates literally to 'Lord of Mictlan'"

"Mitlan is the underground."

"Yes."

"So is he Death?" asks Cale, trying to see where I'm going with this.

"Well, no" I say.

"No?"

"There's this other guy, you've heard of Quexicotl?"

Cale shrugs, "Yes".

"Well he has a twin brother called Xolotl, he's the god of freaks, transformations, duality, life and death, and lighting."

"And this is death?"

"Well he does the same job, it's his job to guide the souls through the journey and their first year in the underworld, he's got the head of a dog."

"I have a friend with a Xoloitzcuintli dog."

"They're named after him," I say. Cale smiles.

"You said you are not wise," he teases, I laugh.

"Since when does knowing a lot make you wise?"

"That's a very wise thing to say," he counters. We both laugh.

"I suppose I'm thinking about Xolotl because one of his main jobs is to carry people over a river in the Underworld at Itzcuintlan. I recently had some problems with water myself." I drain my stein. "Can I buy you another?"

"That would be good," says Cale. Two young kids run through the door.

"Trick or Treat!" they shout in English. One of them is wearing a werewolf mask, the other is dressed like Dracula but has a Lucha wrestling mask on. Before the bar staff react a couple of people sitting nearby hand them some change, and they run out into the night where there's a slight rain misting the streets.

The drinks arrive and me and Cale silently toast. Cale tells me about himself: he builds stages, travels a lot. In the morning he'll help supervise the stage and tents being picked up, and then wait for the next gig. Outside, the rain gets harder and a low rumble and flash comes from outside.

"That's your god again" teases Cale.

"Not my god," I say.

"Are you sure?"

****

Mexico already has a personification of Death; I've done a bit of reading since the tattoo guy told me about her.. Santa Muerte is a folk saint, continuously disavowed by the Catholic Church but worshipped and absorbed into millions of peoples' cosmology just like the old gods hiding behind the cross in the settlers' churches. Mr Death in Mexico isn't a Mr at all. In Spanish, words can be masculine or feminine. 'Death' is feminine: 'LE Meurte'. So, Death in Mexico is a woman.

She's known as the 'narco saint' as she's favoured by people in the drugs trade, but this is perhaps unfair. Death is nothing if not egalitarian, she comes for everyone. She is the saint for the dispossessed, of the people that feel forgotten or unworthy. That particular demographic is growing daily.

The Catholic church is one of splendour and ritual: the Pope sits on a golden throne when most of his subjects sit on plastic chairs. People pray to Santa Muerte for healing, protection, comfort and, yes, swift and painful retribution for those that deserve her wrath. No one really knows where Sainte Meurte worship began, but the first public shrine is generally recognised as being set up by Enriqueta Romero in 2001 in the Teptio neighbourhood here in Mexico City. And with its reputation for robbery, drugs, arm trafficking and other violence, it's perhaps not surprising she found her first home there.

The subway sign for Tepito is a boxing glove in recognition of its history of producing boxing champions, but with its reputation it's hard not to see it as a warning. I jog upstairs and am once again swallowed by a market, clothing stalls mostly. I follow the street, but the market is steel pipes and tarpaulin, racks of branded clothes; Supreme, Nike, Adidas, all knock offs, or stolen, or both. I need to cross the road, but to do that I would have to walk through somebody's stall, and they all seem blocked by either plastic sheeting, displays, or bored looking people on cheap lawn furniture.

I know in my mind that there are buildings here and the market occupies the gaps, but the buildings are strangely missing, crumbling walls, maybe a steel shutter or two is visible. Pop music thumps from six places at once. The stalls have everything: pots and pans, racks and racks of DVDS, screens playing films that I don't think are even out yet in Mexico. CDs with poorly photocopied sleeves. A self defence stall, head guards, punch bags, brass knuckles and nunchucks. Lingerie on headless, shapely plastic golems; branded tech, with the brands smudged. I'm watched wherever I go. I only have a vague idea of the direction I need to go. I do have a map on my phone but I don't want to take it out. When I finally do, it's useless anyway: the maps is of where the buildings and roads are, none of these things exist in the market. The market has been at this site since the Aztecs, the buildings happened while it wasn't looking. I put my phone away and nearly trip on some cables, they lead to a streetlamp with its panel prised off. The market sucks the juice out of the city like it sucks the wealth out of its visitors.

After noticing I'm out from under the tarpaulin I take a chance and free myself by squeezing between stalls towards the road noises. I fall out onto the main road and quickly jog across onto the raised pavement that marks the edge of a neighbourhood consisting of low, one storey buildings. The roads are barely paved with a network of cracks and potholes. The shell of a burnt-out car sits on the corner, smashed and stripped. It's almost obscene, a corpse, ruined and left on display. My hand unconsciously checks my wallet and phone are still in the pockets I left them and then curse myself because

I've just pointed out to anyone watching where I keep my valuables.

A shop is open a little further down the street, I can see by the window that it's a butcher but, to be honest, I could have guessed as soon as I crossed the street and could smell the mixture of blood and flesh. And I'm not the only one, a stray dog sits by the door looking into the dark expectantly. My formative years spent reading The Beano have me picturing the dog sprinting down the road with a string of sausages, chased by a beefy guy with a handlebar moustache. I laugh to myself; the tension and anxiety leave my shoulders. Then at myself for putting myself in this position in the first place.

A short way up the road one of the buildings has an awning. Inside, I spot the candles first and, as I approach, I see her, behind glass. She's about five-foot-tall in the white lace dress of a bride, with a black scarf. The veil has been lifted to show the deep sockets and familiar grin. In her hands is a bouquet, an explosion of white petals and pearls. She stands amongst a lawn of La Catrina statues also in immaculate white, and a row of iridescent silver goblets. Placed in the middle is a baby doll in christening robes, eyes deader than Our Lady's could ever be. To the right, there a plastic table and chairs with a woven table cloth. An older woman and a man in a crumpled suit are sitting there. She is holding one of his hands in both of hers, his eyes are red and he's talking fast, his voice hitching. It seems like an intensely private moment, neither pause or acknowledge my presence.

I switch my attention to the offerings in front of Our Lady. Candles are lit, there are four or five cigarettes, two of which are burning to ash. There're shot glasses filled with what smells like tequila as well as a couple of open beer cans. Tucked between all this are pieces of paper with what I can make out to be finely handwritten script. I let go of a deep breath and take a look at Our Lady's face. She's Death, but not mine. She wouldn't answer my questions even if she knew the answers. That's okay though. I'm standing in one of the roughest neighborhoods in possibly the world's biggest city and I feel calm. But that's the thing with Our Lady, her face can be anything: angry to the wrathful, solace to the mournful, and calm to the dumb white guy poking around where he shouldn't. I don't light a candle because they're not mine to light. But I do leave offerings on her altar. I leave my quest, the broken version of me that needed it so badly, and for good measure I leave a secret, that's for me and her alone.

The market is getting sketchy. I've ducked down an alley because I felt the hairs on my neck prickle with the eyes fixed on my back and I wanted to get back to the main road quickly. Here the stalls are less frequent, just the bare skeleton. A lot of young people are hanging around. What stalls there are are sex or pot related, dusty dildos in opened packages next to glass pipes or boxes of sun faded rizlas. As I walk past I get "weed", "coke" hissed into my ear. I hear an engine and instinctively step out of the way as a moped screams past. The DVDs on the stalls are increasingly photocopied, until they're just clear plastic folders with neon sales stickers advertising 'Besitalie' 'snuf 100% real' and even 'necrofila (real)'. I'm being grabbed now. Lightly at first, just to catch my attention "weed", "coke", "weedcoke".

But the grabs are getting firmer, holding me until I have to force myself out of their grip. I need to get out of there now, but I know if I run I'm prey, even more of a target. I force myself to straighten up to my full height and walk towards the sunlight. Whenever I'm grabbed I pull away firmly and even though I want to say 'NO' firmly, it's filtered through years of Englishness and comes out

"NO… thank you."

I get to the main road and the mood of the market shifts. I'm safe, but I don't dawdle back to the station.

****

I leave tomorrow and I'm upstairs in the hostel's smoking area. The whole floor is open plan with wicker furniture next to huge windows that take up three sides of the square space. I'm told in the summer this space is used for parties but in the dead time it sits fairly dormant. I've turned the lights off and I'm watching the traffic and the night unfold while doing a mental checklist of tomorrow's journey back. When I get to my passport I browse the conversation with Rita on my phone. Fine, fine… then I get to the part about the visa. I forgot I'd have to buy a replacement visa. Okay, I've got a bit of money, but I don't know how much it'll cost. And, thinking about it, there's nothing left on the travel debit card account. No problem, I'll just transfer some from my actual bank account. Done. I check my travelcard account and it hasn't been processed yet. Fine I'll just give it half an hour? Half an hour later it's still not in. Shouldn't it be instantaneous? I've always transferred money with plenty of time before. Maybe it processes at the end of the day, at twelve. I sit for another hour. Well after twelve, still not in. Okay I've got cash and anyway, it'll probably be in at the start of the next working day right?

Wrong. I'm checking out, I hand the key over and the smiling clerk says

"Aaaand we just have to settle your account."

"What do you mean? I paid up front?"

"Well there is a note here saying there's a deficit."

"How much?"

"1,386 peso."

"Can you please go check because I paid quite a lot to begin with," I say. She smiles and goes to speak to the management. She comes back with the books and the receipt that I'd signed. There is a deficit.

"Shit."

In the subway station waiting for my connecting train, the 5 pesos for the barrier was the last of my money, so I can't leave to get a taxi, or even another subway. I'm still checking the travelcard website waiting for the transferred money to clear, which is taking my mind off the fact that time is ticking down and every train so far has been the special type of full that requires physically pushing people tighter together and praying your dick bulge clears the closing doors. In turn, this is taking my mind off the fact I have no money to pay for the official paperwork I need to leave the country. There is no way of getting on with a rucksack without pulling people out beforehand. The first two or three trains that come I let go with a smile, they'll be less busy soon I've told myself. Now, the sixth train has gone past with the same level of compression. I need to get on soon and it's becoming increasingly likely it'll involve holding my rucksack in front of me and charging the train like a linebacker because I can't be late to buy a visa with my zero money.

The seventh train comes, still unreasonably full, but I notice that no one is getting on and off at the top of the platform. Hefting my bag, I wait at the very edge. Train number eight arrives and the end car is still full, but not insanely so. I shoulder my way on and push my rucksack against the driver's cabin door, leaning over it, trying to take up as little floor space as necessary.

Mexico City International is nice. I know it's nice because I've walked the length of it three or four times looking for the immigration office. My annoyance is tempered by apprehension - I have no money still but I've decided to play dumb. I'll hand over my bank card and, when it doesn't go through, look shocked and confused, hurt even. I mean, there has to be some sort of proviso for this, they can't make me miss my flight right? Surely it is in everyone's best interest to bundle as many idiot tourists who lose important paperwork out of the country as quickly as possible before they do themselves a mischief? We'll find out, I suppose.

I find the office, they speak English so I explain about my stolen passport and visa, waiting for the admonishment for not replacing it immediately. But none comes. Just a form. While I fill out the form I mentally practice my shocked face. 'Declined? Wow, really?'.

The lady comes over and checks my form.

"Are you okay?" she asks, concerned.

"Yes," I say.

"It's just you were making a face," she says.

"I was just… thinking."

The lady looks my form over, I get my card in my hand. She stamps the form twice, rips it in half and gives me part of it to put in my passport. I wait for her to tell me how much. But nothing happens.

"Soooo," I don't want to bring up money in case they remember. "I'll just go now I suppose," I say.

"Have a nice flight," she says but maintains eye contact. Is she waiting for me to offer to pay? Is this a trick? I back away still smiling. I reach my backpack, put it on and turn, waiting for a hand on my shoulder or a shout. None comes.

I float through security and check-in with a relief that is tangible, so pure I can barely string a sentence together. At the gate I try to buy a bottle of water with some coins I found at the bottom of my bag but don't have enough money. The lady at the checkout takes my change and shows me a bottle of orange drink I can afford, and before I know it I'm in the air.

I'm on the roof again, sober - ish. The spring afternoon has chilled enough for my fingers to get increasingly stiff while I methodically untie the knots from my newly clean marionette puppet. I'm fumbling between sips of rum. The sun sets to the left and I occasionally take a few moments to feel the warmth on my face and the slight difference in temperature between each side. Señor Carpenter is looking better. I just need to disassemble him a little to fix the knots and twists in his strings. His grinning face reminds me of my mission.

Did I find Death? No. Well, maybe. Death found me, a few of them did, actually. But looking back that wasn't really why I went. The urge to escape is normal: run away to be someone or something else. Someone less damaged, in less pain. But in the words of Buckaroo Banzai, noted physicist, neuroscientist, test pilot and rock star 'wherever you go, there you are'. Your bullshit, your pain, is there waiting, just after baggage claim. In the same way, when I do die my dog headed friend, or powerful bride, or skeleton in the hood will be there. And I'll be happy for the help.

There's a story I heard while researching Death, it's about the first human. Now, this probably wasn't the first person because people lived for a long time back then, but they were definitely the first human, because they were the first person to die. And it's the dying that gives our stories shape, death makes us human. But they were scared. Dying is scary now, but back then no one had ever done it before, so the first human is dead and alone and very scared. So they walked, searching for what happens next, searching for a path, a trail. For so long the first human discovered you can be bored and scared at the same time. Eventually they found what we'll call 'heaven' for now.

"Welcome," said the guy on the door, eager to meet his first booking.

"Thanks," the first human said, "where am I?"

"Oh," said the doorman. "This is heaven, you're the first, but there will be many others. Come in, an eternity of peace and pleasure and fulfilment awaits"

"Oh…erm…No, thank you," said the first human.

"You're very wel…wait what?" said the doorman, this is off script.

"No thank you," the first human repeated.

"Where are you going to go, there is nowhere else?" spluttered the doorman who's first day on the job is not going how he expects.

"Well," said the first, "I was so scared and so lost and no one should have to do that alone, so I think I'm going to stick around and show people the way."

And so they did.

The End

Danny Smith is a writer, degenerate, and malcontent. He has done lots of things for money: he has worked behind, and on the doors of, some of the roughest pubs in Birmingham, he sold CD-ROMs door-to-door in the suburbs of one of the most isolated cities in the world, he's wrestled children of various sizes, taught kids from the ghettos of New Jersey how to shoot a bow, talked down the strung-out at various festivals, and protected people against nightmares.

Being a ferocious reader in his younger years Danny didn't really start taking writing seriously until he was dropping out of his Fine Art degree in his 20s, since then he's been published in various magazine including Vice, Area, and Fused, published three small press books and Pier Review, where he and co-conspirator, Jon Bounds visited all 55 pleasure piers in England and Wales in two weeks, published by Summersdale

Acknowledgements

Books are not easy, the fact you have this one in your hands is down to these people. So I need to thank; JON BOUNDS, as good an editor/publisher/designer/typesetter as he is a friend (not a backhanded compliment), MAT ATKINS for proofing what must have been several hundred pages of nonsense, BEN WHITEHOUSE for the most joyous live commentary on a test reading anyone could hope for, and LUCY CHAMBERS for everything else. If you enjoyed any of this book it is down to these people, any mistakes you spot are entirely my own…

Printed in Great Britain
by Amazon